Top 25 locator map
(continues on inside
back cover)

◄

CityPack
Rome

TIM JEPSON

If you have any comments
or suggestions for this guide
you can contact the editor at
CityPack@theAA.com

AA Publishing
Find out more about AA Publishing and the
wide range of services the AA provide by
visiting our website at *www.theAA.com*

About this Book

ORGANIZATION

This guide is divided into six sections:

- Planning Ahead and Getting There
- Living Rome—Rome Now, Rome Then, Time to Shop, Out and About, Walks, Rome by Night
- Rome's Top 25 Sights
- Rome's Best—best of the rest
- Where to—detailed listings of restaurants, hotels, shops and nightlife
- Travel facts—packed with practical information

In addition, easy-to-read side panels provide extra facts and snippets, highlights of places to visit and invaluable practical advice.

The colours of the tabs on the page corners match the colours of the triangles aligned with the chapter names on the contents page opposite.

MAPS

The fold-out map in the wallet at the back of the book is a comprehensive street plan of Rome. The first (or only) map reference given for each attraction refers to this map. **The Top 25 locator maps** found on the inside front and back covers of the book itself are for quick reference. They show the Top 25 Sights, described on pages 26–50, which are clearly plotted by number (**1**–**25**, not page number) across the city. The second map reference given for the Top 25 Sights refers to this map.

Contents

Planning Ahead

WHEN TO GO

The best time to visit Rome is April to early June or mid-September to October, when the weather is not uncomfortably hot. Easter weekend is very busy. Many restaurants and businesses close for the entire month of August. January and February are the quietest months.

TIME

Italy is one hour ahead of GMT in winter, six hours ahead of New York and nine hours ahead of Los Angeles.

AVERAGE DAILY MAXIMUM TEMPERATURES

JAN	FEB	MAR	APR	MAY	JUN	JUL	AUG	SEP	OCT	NOV	DEC
44°F	46°F	52°F	58°F	64°F	74°F	79°F	77°F	72°F	64°F	55°F	48°F
7°C	8°C	11°C	14°C	18°C	23°C	26°C	25°C	22°C	18°C	13°C	9°C

Spring (March to April) can be muggy and rainy in April and May.
Summer (June to August) is hot and dry, with sudden thunderstorms. July and August are uncomfortably hot.
Autumn (September to November) is mixed but can produce crisp days with clear skies.
Winter (December to February) is short and cold.

WHAT'S ON

January *La Befana* (6 Jan): Epiphany celebrations; fair and market in Piazza Navona.
February *Carnevale* (week before Lent): Costume festivities; parties on Shrove Tuesday.
March *Festa di San Giuseppe* (19 Mar): Street stalls in the Trionfale area north of the Vatican.
April *Good Friday* (Mar/Apr): Procession of the Cross at 9pm to the Colosseum, led by the Pope.
Easter Sunday: The Pope addresses the crowds at noon in Piazza di San Pietro.

May *International Horse Show* (early May): Concorso Ippico in Villa Borghese.
June *Festa della Repubblica* (2 Jun): Military parade along Via de' Fiori Imperiali.
July *Tevere Expo* (last week Jun/Jul): Food and handi-crafts fair on the banks of the Tiber.
August *Ferragosto* (15 Aug): Feast of the Assumption; everything closes.
September *Art Fair*: Via Margutta.
Sagra dell'Uva (early Sep): Wine and harvest festival in the Basilica di Massenzio.

October *Antiques Fair* (mid-Oct): Via dei Coronari.
November *Ognissanti* (1–2 Nov): All Saints' Day. *Festa di Santa Cecilia* (22 Nov): In the catacombs and church of Santa Cecilia in Trastavere.
December *Festa della Madonna Immacolata* (8 Dec): Pope and other dignitaries leave flowers at the statue of the Madonna in Piazza di Spagna.
Christmas Eve Midnight Mass: Most striking are at Santa Maria Maggiore and Santa Maria in Aracoeli.

ROME ONLINE

www.romaturismo.it
Rome's official website for tourist information, contains mostly generalised information on the city.

www.enjoyrome.com
Another useful tourist information site with material on accommodation, city tours and a range of links to other Rome sites.

www.vatican.va
Vatican City's polished official website offers multilingual information on the Musei Vaticani (► 27), a calendar of religious events, an online version of its official newspaper and other general information on the Vatican.

www.comune.roma.it
Aimed primarily at tourists, the official website of Rome's city council contains transport and other useful general information.

www.romaclick.com
A big, general site useful for checking up-to-the-minute information on events and exhibitions. It offers a user-friendly accommodation reservation service with last-minute reductions.

www.romeguide.it
An Italian-based site with a wealth of daily updated information; use it for reserving museum passes and to find out what's on.

www.enjoyrome.com
This friendly English-language site is run from Rome and has a quirkier approach than most; use it for general information, as well as tips on discovering Rome on foot and by public transport. Excellent links and daily updates.

www.museionline.it
This informative and easy-to-navigate site will fill you in on the crème de la crème the city's museums have to offer—plenty of practical information as well.

PRIME TRAVEL SITES

www.atac.roma.it
Rome's bus company website gives every scrap of information about public transport, including maps and how to buy the best ticket for your needs—Italian and English.

www.capitolium.org
Devoted to the Roman Forum and the Imperial Fora, this site includes a wide range of historical material, including reconstructions of how the Fora might have looked in its original state.

www.catacombe.roma.it
The official site of Rome's catacombs.

www.fodors.com
A travel-planning site where you can research prices and weather, book tickets, cars and rooms, and ask questions; links to other sites.

CYBERCAFÉS
Rimaweb
✉ Via del Portico d'Ottavia 2a ☎ 06 6889 1356; www.rimaweb.com
🕐 Mon–Fri 9.30–6.30/7.30

Globalservice
✉ Piazza S Sonnino 27
☎ 06 5833 3316
🕐 Daily 8am–midnight

and Getting There

BEFORE YOU GO

All visitors to Italy require a valid passport. Visas are not required for UK, New Zealand, US, Canadian, Irish or Australian citizens, or other EU nationals staying fewer than three months. Private medical insurance is advised–EU nationals receive reduced cost medical treatment with a qualifying document (Form E111 for Britons).

MONEY

The euro is the official currency of Italy. Banknotes in denominations of 5, 10, 20, 50, 100, 200 and 500 euros and coins in denominations of 1, 2, 5, 10, 20, 50 cents and 1 and 2 euros were introduced on 1 January 2002.

€50

€200

€500

ARRIVING

There are direct flights into Rome from Europe and North America to Leonardo da Vinci and Ciampino airports. Visitors from Europe can also arrive by rail to Stazione Termini, or by bus.

60KM (37 MILES)

Leonardo da Vinci Airport
36km (22 miles) to city centre
Train 45 minutes, €8.80

Ciampino Airport
15km (9 miles) to city centre
Bus/Metro 35 minutes

FROM LEONARDO DA VINCI

Scheduled flights arrive at this airport 36km (22 miles) southwest of the city centre, better known as Fiumicino (☎ 06 6595 3640/4455). Heavy volume of air traffic usually means you can face congestion and delays. The most economical way to reach the centre of Rome from the airport is by rail into Stazione Termini. Trains leave every 30 or 60 minutes (6.30am–11.30pm) and take roughly 35 minutes. Buses depart outside train hours and take up to 50 minutes to Rome's Tiburtina railway station. Taxis can take from 30 minutes up to two hours depending on traffic, and are expensive (€40–55). Take only licensed cabs (white or yellow) or a pre-paid, car with driver' available from the SOCAT desk in the International Arrivals hall.

FROM CIAMPINO

This smaller airport, which handles mostly low-cost and charter flights, is 15km (9 miles) southeast of the city centre. There are good facilities but the airport doesn't have a direct link to the centre of Rome. To get there you will need to take a 15-minute bus journey by COTRAL bus to the Metro (underground) station at Anagnina, then the 20-minute journey to Termini on Metro line A. Taxis take between 30 and 40 minutes and cost around €26.

Arriving by Rail

Most trains arrive and depart from Stazione Termini, which is convenient for most of central Rome. Taxis and buses leave from the station forecourt, Piazza dei Cinquecento. Train information ☎ 8488 88088; www.fs-on-line.com.

Getting Around

Service is frequent and inexpensive on Rome's orange, green or red-grey regional and suburban buses run by COTRAL. The buses are often crowded and slow. Buy tickets before boarding, which are available from tobacconists, automatic machines, shops, and newsstands displaying an ATAC sticker. Your ticket must be stamped at the rear of the bus or tram, and is valid for any number of bus rides and one Metro ride within the next 75 minutes. There are large fines if you are caught without a ticket. Daytime services run from 5.30am to 11.30pm. The night service consists of 23 buses on key routes from midnight to 5.30am. Unlike day buses, night buses have a conductor selling tickets.

Rome's subway system, the Metro, has two lines, A and B, which intersect at Stazione Termini. Primarily a commuter service and of only limited use in the city centre, it is good for quick transcity rides. Station entrances are marked by a large red M and each displays a map of the network. Services run from 5.30am to 11.30pm (12.30am on Saturdays). Tickets are valid for one ride and can be bought from tobacconists, bars and shops displaying ATAC or COTROL stickers, and from machines at stations.

Official taxis are yellow or white, with a 'Taxi' sign on the roof. Use only these and refuse touts at Fiumicino, Termini and elsewhere. Drivers are not supposed to stop on the streets so it is difficult to hail a cab. Taxis congregate at stands, indicated by blue signs printed with *Taxi*. Make sure the meter is at zero when you start your journey. For more on public transport ➤ 90–91.

HANDY HINT

An integrated ticket, the *Biglietto Integrato* (BIG) is valid for a day's unlimited travel on ATAC buses, the Metro, COTRAL buses and suburban railways (except to Fiumicino airport). The *Carta Integrata Settimanale* pass is valid for a week; services as for BIG tickets.

VISITORS WITH DISABILITIES

Rome is not an easy place for visitors with physical disabilities. However, Vatican City has ramps and elevators and some hotels have rooms for visitors with disabilities. Staff at airports, museums and places of interest are willing to help and taxis usually accept wheelchairs, although it is a good idea to phone ahead. The B line metro is generally accessible (apart from Circo Massimo, Colosseo and Cavour) but the A line and most buses are not. For details contact RADAR (✉ Unit 12, City Forum, 250 City Road, London ECU 8AF ☎ 020 7250 3222) in the UK or Society for the Advancement of Travel and Hospitality (SATH) (✉ 347 Fifth Avenue, NY 10006 ☎ 212/447 7284; www.sath.com) in the US.

Living
Rome

Rome Now

Above: *One of many pretty street cafés in Piazza Navona*
Top right: *The Colosseum, spectacularly lit up at night*
Right: *The banks of the River Tiber, away from the constant throng of people in the city*

Rome is one of the most romantic places in the world. Soaked in the culture and history of centuries, it is the city of the Caesars, of languorous sunny days and *la dolce vita*, of art and endless galleries, of religion, churches and museums, of fountain-splashed piazzas and majestic monuments to its golden age of empire. In addition, it has the seductions of any Italian destination—notably superb food and wine—as well as the wide-ranging attractions of a modern world capital: great bars and cafés, excellent shopping, a vibrant nightlife and a lively calendar of cultural events.

Here, more than in most cities, the historic city is also the contemporary city: Traffic rumbles around medieval cobbled streets, ancient monuments form the fabric of many everyday houses and the skyline bristles not with glittering skyscrapers but with the towers and domes of churches and palaces.

Above: *The Pantheon's dome is one of the marvels of Roman engineering*
Left: *Taking stock outside the Pantheon*

SECRET KEYHOLE

• Rome's most charming view is from Piazza dei Cavalieri di Malta on the Aventine Hill southwest of the Colosseum. To find it, walk to the left of the church of Santa Sabina (as you face the church), perhaps after looking briefly in the lovely gardens to the church's right. Continue to the end of the piazza and look through the keyhole of the huge door (No. 3) of the Priory of the Knights of Malta. Through the tiny hole you will see a secret garden and an avenue of trees cleverly framing…but let's not spoil the surprise: Go and see for yourself.

WATERY WASTE

• More than 50 of Rome's fountains are fed by the waters of the Aqua Virgo, a source that the Romans first brought into the city in 19BC. It flows from the countryside outside the city, and feeds the Barcaccia fountain at the foot of the Spanish Steps, before supplying many others, including the most famous of them all, the Fontana di Trevi.

Above: *The Fountain of the Four Rivers at the heart of Piazza Navona*

Not that the past is preserved as in a museum. Rome has seen countless changes over the centuries, and in the period leading up to the millennium—a special Holy Year in the city that saw many millions of extra visitors and pilgrims—numerous churches, palaces, monuments and galleries received a facelift. This extra work meant that much of the city now presents a more gleaming than usual face to the world.

Rome's museums and galleries are also undergoing something of a renaissance. The city's Roman monuments have often been closed to the public, and its great art displayed in dated or lacklustre settings. Much has changed in this regard, and will change further as other projects come to fruition. Newer galleries such as the Palazzo Altemps and Palazzo Massimo alle Terme are wonderful and modern, displaying classical art and sculpture in beautiful period buildings. Now open after decades are parts of the Palazzo Barberini and the Domus Aurea, Nero's Golden House, close to the Colosseum.

Although Rome is a city immersed in the past, it must also function in the present. As a result,

AMBASSADORS AND ENVOYS

• Most countries are represented in Rome both in the Italian State and in the Vatican, an independent state. Representatives to the Vatican have their offices scattered about the city as space is limited within Vatican City itself. They have full diplomatic status, as do the Pope's envoys throughout the world.

Above: *Church domes and spires dominate the evening sky*
Left: *Elderly Romans enjoy a chat surrounded by the splendour of Piazza Navona*

it can be a city of unsettling extremes. The noise and heavy traffic in busy periods, for example, can be striking and unexpected, as can the sheer number of people—locals and visitors—crammed into the streets and museums. Tackle the city without bearing this in mind, and in the heat of a summer afternoon, and you may emerge the worse for wear, battered rather than enraptured.

DEATH RATTLE

• San Giovanni in Laterano (► 50) contains a monument to Pope Sylvester II that reputedly sweats and makes the sound of rattling bones prior to the death of a pope.

KNOW YOUR STREETS

• Visitors to Rome are often baffled by the dates that make up many street names. Here's a breakdown of what they mean:

• **Via XXV Aprile (25 April)** The date Rome was liberated by Allied forces in 1944.

• **Via XXIV Maggio (24 May)** The day Italy declared war on Austria in 1915.

• **Via XX Settembre (20 September)** The day Italian troops liberated Rome from papal and French forces in 1870.

• **Via IV Novembre (4 November)** The date of the Italian armistice and victory in 1918 after World War I.

Right: *Swiss Guards at the Vatican*
Above: *The elegant spiral staircase at the entrance to the Vatican Museums*

SWISS GUARD

• The pope's official bodyguards are recruited from Switzerland's four predominantly Catholic cantons. Each must be between 19 and 25, at least 1.75cm (5ft 8in) tall and remain unmarried during their tour of duty. Their distinctive uniforms were designed by Michelangelo in the colours of the Medici popes—red, yellow and blue.

To uncover the city at its most beguiling, therefore, don't try to do too much. At least initially forgo big-name sights like St. Peter's and the Colosseum. Instead start with a stroll around the Ghetto or Trastevere, two of the city's quaintest old quarters, or have a quiet cappuccino in one or other of its loveliest squares, Campo de' Fiori or Piazza Navona. Alternatively, wander into some of the city's greener corners such as the Villa Borghese and Pincio Gardens. Better still, start with one of the lesser-known churches, such as beautiful San Clemente, with its multi-layered monuments to pagan and medieval Rome, or Santa Maria del Popolo, crammed with masterpieces by Raphael, Pinturicchio and Caravaggio.

Then you can begin to explore a city that mingles its magnificent past with a sometimes brash present. But don't focus only on the city's history. Contemporary pleasures include shopping—this is a great place for antiques,

clothes, accessories, shoes, leatherware and craft items—or sample the food. Food in Rome has always been hearty rather than sophisticated, and in the past has had the generally simple, trattoria-style restaurants to match. However, a sprinkling of modern restaurants and bars have opened, taking note of the more contemporary food, style and up-to-the-minute design of new restaurants in cities such as London and New York.

Nor should you ignore the lifeblood of any great metropolis—its inhabitants. In Rome they are as startling and individual as their city. Romans have had to develop thick skins to deal with the stresses and strains of living in a city sometimes cramped by its past—not to mention the floodtide of tourists that further burdens its overstretched resources. This said, a smile and a little stuttered Italian usually brings courtesy instead of gruffness and you should revel in the city's almost Fellini-esque cast of characters, from the pot-bellied restaurateurs and dog-walking old women to fallen aristocrats, grumpy bartenders and rough-fingered market matriarchs.

Above: *Outside the Vatican Museums*

ROMAN HILLS

● Rome is built on seven hills, which still retain their Roman names: Palatine, Celian, Capitoline, Aventine, Quirinal, Esquiline and Viminal. The Palatine, home of the emperors, gave us the word 'palace', while the Capitoline, seat of the government, is remembered in 'capital' cities throughout the world. Visitors must toil up and down these hills when exploring Rome, but it may feel like more than seven as Rome actually spreads over 20 hills.

15

Rome Then

Above: Murder
of Caesar by
Karl Theodor
von Piloty, 1865

PUNIC WARS

The First Punic War
against Carthage (North
Africa) started in 264BC
and lasted for around 23
years. In the Second
Punic War (218–201BC)
Rome was threatened by
Hannibal, leader of the
Carthaginian army. But
Rome finally defeated
Carthage in the Third
Punic War (149–146BC).

RELIGION

There are 280 churches
within the city walls and
94 per cent of Romans
have had their children
baptized. However, only
23 per cent of Romans
attend Mass. Forty per
cent of Romans favour
women priests; the same
number believe in hell.

753BC Traditional date of the foundation of Rome by Romulus, first of the city's seven kings.

616– 578BC Tarquinius Priscus, Rome's first Etruscan king.

509BC Etruscans expelled and the Republic founded.

60BC Rome ruled by a triumvirate of Pompey, Marcus Licinius Crassus and Julius Caesar.

48BC Caesar declared ruler for life but assassinated by rivals in 44BC.

27BC– AD14 Rule of Octavian, Caesar's great nephew, who as Augustus becomes the first Roman emperor.

AD42 St. Peter the Apostle visits Rome.

72 The Colosseum is begun.

98–117 Reign of Emperor Trajan. Military campaigns greatly extend the Empire's boundaries.

284–286 Empire divided into East and West.

306–337 The Emperor Constantine reunites the Empire and legalises Christianity. St. Peter's and the first Christian churches are built.

410 Rome is sacked by the Goths.

476 Romulus Augustulus is the last Roman Emperor.

800 Charlemagne awards some territories to papacy; Pope Leo III crowns him Holy Roman Emperor.

1452–1626 The construction of a new St. Peter's begins and spans over 150 years.

1508 Michelangelo begins the Sistine Chapel ceiling.

1527 Rome is sacked and looted by German and Spanish troops under Charles V.

1848 Uprisings in Rome under Mazzini and Garibaldi force Pope Pius IX to flee. The new 'Roman Republic' is ultimately defeated by the French.

1870 Rome joins a united Italy.

1929 The Lateran Treaty recognises the Vatican as a separate state.

1940 Italy enters World War II.

1960 Rome hosts the Olympic Games.

2000 Some 30 million pilgrims visit Rome for the millennial jubilee year.

Left to right: A view of the city, carved in wood in 1493; a 19th-century engraving of St. Peter's, by G. Lago; Benito Mussolini; the emblem of the Rome Olympics

VITAL STATISTICS

• The official age of Rome (in 2003) is 2,756 years.
• There have been 168 popes and 73 emperors.
• The number of vestal virgins at any one time was six.
• The length of service of a vestal virgin was 30 years.
• The area of the city covers 1494sq km (577sq miles).
• The city is 27km (17 miles) from the sea.
• The amount of water delivered by aqueducts to Rome in the 2nd century AD was 68,640L (312,000 gal).
• The estimated number of tourists annually is 15 million.

17

Time to Shop

Above: *Central Rome's biggest general market near Piazza Vittorio Emanuele II*

ANTIQUES

It is no wonder, given Rome's long history, that the city is a treasury of antiques. Prices are often high, but the range of artefacts—Etruscan, Roman, Renaissance, baroque and other items—is unrivalled. For paintings and prints, head for Via Margutta, which also has a scattering of galleries selling contemporary art and carpets, while for general antiques try Via Giulia, Via del Babuino (particularly for Persian carpets), Via del Coronari, Via dell'Orso and Via del Monserrato. Also good, and with lower prices and less exclusive stock, are Via de Panico, Via del Pellegrino and Via dei Banchi Nuovi.

Rome was once the market place of an empire that embraced much of the known world. These days it has a more humble place in the shopping firmament. This said, all the great Italian retail staples—food, wine, fashion, shoes, leatherware and clothing—are well represented, and the city is a good source of art, antiques, traditional crafts and artisan products such as furniture.

Mid-priced shoes and clothes represent good value for money; you will find them in countless shops around the new city, but particularly Via Nazionale, Via del Tritone and Via del Corso. The same streets are also dotted with small specialist shops selling good quality bags, gloves and other leatherware. The sprawling Piazza Vittorio Emanuele market, where most Romans do their shopping, is also a good source of clothes and shoes, as well as pots, pans and kitchenware with an Italian stamp (such as coffee-makers).

At the other sartorial extreme, most of the great Italian and European fashion houses have shops in the city: Gucci, Prada, Armani, Versace are all here, mostly in the grid of streets around Via Condotti, an excellent source of high-class

Left to right: *Colourful market stalls and the atmospheric bustle in the tight labyrinth of busy streets can be one of Rome's most enduring memories*

clothes, shoes, lingerie and accessories. Department stores have not really caught on, and only Coin and Rinascente are worth a visit.

Shopping for food has a unique charm in Rome, whether in the small neighbourhood shops known as *alimentari*, or the specialist delicatessens in streets such as Via della Croce. The city's ancient markets, particularly Campo de' Fiori, are colourful sources for provisions.

The range of shops selling ecclesiastical items is vast. The largest concentration is around St. Peter's, notably on Borgo Pio and Via della Conciliazione—look out for ceramic Swiss Guards and fluorescent rosaries. On Via dei Cestari all manner of ecclesiastic garb is available—if you ever daydreamed about buying a bishop's robe or a cardinal's hat, this is the place.

Finally, Rome has any number of shops and stalls selling plaster and plastic casts of famous statues. Better quality items, plus books, prints, T-shirts and artistic replicas, can be found in museum and gallery shops.

MARBLED PAPER

Notebooks and other stationery items covered with marbled paper make wonderful souvenirs, which you can find in shops all over the city. The paper originated in Venice, where the technique arrived from the east in the 15th century, and is still handmade. The process involves floating multi-coloured pigments on liquid gum and combing the different colours, separated by ox-gall, into distinctive patterns. The paper is placed delicately on top, then lifted and hung up to dry.

19

Out & About

Left to right: Campo de' Fiori; fountains are the highlight of Villa d'Este, Tivoli; an important archaeological site, Ostia Antica

AMERICAN EXPRESS

American Express runs bus tours around Rome, Tivoli and farther afield. It also organizes three- to four-hour walks of the city with English-speaking guides: the Vatican City tour, Rome of the Caesars', and 'Religious Rome', which visits the Catacombs, Pantheon, Piazza Navona and St. Peter's. Reservations are advisable at busy times.

✉ Piazza di Spagna 38
☎ 06 67642
🕐 Mon–Fri 9–5.30, Sat 9–3, Apr–Sep; Mon–Fri 9–5.30, Sat 9–12.30, rest of year
🚇 Spagna
🚌 119 to Piazza di Spagna

ITINERARIES

ANCIENT ROME

After breakfast at an outdoor café in Campo de' Fiori (➤ 31), stroll through the Ghetto district towards Santa Maria in Aracoeli (➤ 40) and the Capitoline Museums (➤ 39). Near by, you have the choice of the Roman Forum and the Palatine (➤ 43), and the Colosseum (➤ 45) to explore, or the Arch of Constantine (➤ 52) to admire.

For lunch you could picnic in the Parco Oppio (➤ 58). Then it's on to the churches of San Pietro in Vincoli (➤ 46), San Clemente (➤ 48) and San Giovanni in Laterano (➤ 50). From here take the Metro to Termini for Santa Maria Maggiore (➤ 49).

PANTHEON TO ST. PETER'S

Start the day with breakfast in Piazza della Rotonda, before visiting the nearby Pantheon (➤ 35), Santa Maria sopra Minerva (➤ 36) and San Luigi dei Francesi (➤ 32). Move on to Piazza Navona (➤ 32) for morning coffee and then take a short stroll across the bridge to Castel Sant' Angelo (➤ 29). Stop for a picnic lunch in the Parco Andriano.

From here you can spend the early afternoon visiting the Vatican Museums (➤ 27), Sistine Chapel (➤ 28) and St. Peter's (➤ 26). Complete the day by taking a short walk south towards Trastevere where you can enjoy an evening meal at one of Rome's best fish restaurants, Alberto Ciarla (➤ 64), or at the more modest Augusto (➤ 66).

EXCURSIONS
OSTIA ANTICA

Untrumpeted Ostia Antica, 25km (15 miles) southwest of Rome, is Italy's best-preserved Roman town after Pompeii and Herculaneum, its extensive ruins and lovely rural site are as appealing as any in Rome itself. Built at the mouth (*ostium*) of the Tiber as ancient Rome's seaport, it became a vast and bustling colony before silt and the Empire's decline together hastened its demise. Among the many excavated buildings are countless *horrea*, or warehouses, and several multi-storey apartment blocks known as *insulae*. Other highlights include the Pazzale delle Corporazioni (the old business district) and the 4,000-seat amphitheatre.

TIVOLI

Tivoli is the most popular excursion from Rome, thanks to the town's lovely wooded position, the superlative gardens of the Villa d'Este and the ruins and grounds of Hadrian's Roman villa. The Este gardens were laid out in 1550 as part of a country retreat for Cardinal Ippolito d'Este, son of Lucrezia Borgia and the Duke of Ferrara. The highlights among the beautifully integrated terraces and many fountains are Gian Lorenzo Bernini's elegant Fontana di Bicchierone and the vast Viale delle Cento Fontane ('Avenue of the Hundred Fountains'). Hadrian's Villa, the largest ever conceived in the Roman world, was built between AD118 and 135 and covered an area as great as the centre of imperial Rome.

INFORMATION

OSTIA ANTICA
Distance 25km (15 miles)
Journey time 35 minutes
✉ Viale di Romagnoli 717
☎ 06 5635 8099
🕐 Tue–Sun 9–6, Apr–Sep; Tue–Sun 9–4, rest of year (last entry 60–90 minutes before closing). Closed holidays
🚇 Metro line B to Piramide, then trains from adjoining railway station every 10–30 minutes (covered by BIG ticket ➤ 7)
🍴 Moderate

TIVOLI
Distance 31km (19 miles)
Journey time 40 minutes
🚆 Train to Tivoli from Termini
🚌 COTRAL bus from Via Goeta or metro line B to Ponte Mammolo and then COTRAL bus to Tivoli
Villa d'Este
✉ Piazza Trento
☎ 0774 312070
🕐 Tue–Sun 9–7.30, Apr–Sep (until one hour before dusk rest of year)
🍴 Expensive
Villa Adriana
✉ Via Tiburtino
☎ 0774 530203
🕐 Daily 9–6.30, May–Aug (until one hour before dusk rest of year)
🚌 Local bus No. 4 from Tivoli
🍴 Moderate

Walks

INFORMATION

Time 2–4 hours
Distance 4.5km (3 miles)
Start point ★
Piazza Venezia
➕ fIII; D6
🚌 40, 44, 46, 60, 61, 64, 70, 81, 87, 170
End point St. Peter's
➕ bII; B5
🚌 40 or 64 to Largo di Torre Argentina, Piazza Venezia, Termini
🚇 See Capitoline Museums and churches first (most close noon). The Castel Sant' Angelo may be shut when you arrive. St. Peter's closes 7pm (summer), 6pm (winter)
🍴 Trastè (➤ 70)

FROM PIAZZA VENEZIA TO ST. PETER'S THROUGH THE HISTORIC CITY CENTRE AND TRASTEVERE

Start at Piazza Venezia. Take Via del Teatro di Marcello to the steps of Piazza del Campidoglio. At the south corner of the piazza, Via del Campidoglio leads to a view over the Forum, then to Via della Consolazione and Santa Maria in Cosmedin. From Piazza della Consolazione walk south to Piazza Bocca della Verità. Follow Lungotevere dei Pierleoni north along the river, and cross Ponte Fabricio to Isola Tiberina.

Cross Ponte Cestio and follow Via Anicia south to Santa Cecilia in Trastevere. Cut northwest to Viale di Trastevere and Piazza Sidney Sonnino, and follow Via della Lungaretta west to Piazza Santa Maria in Trastevere. Leave the piazza to the north, towards Vicolo dei Cinque and Piazza Trilussa. Cross the Ponte Sisto, follow Via dei Pettinari northeast, and turn northwest on Via Capo di Ferro to Piazza Farnese and Campo de' Fiori. Take Via dei Cappellari northwest from Campo de' Fiori, turn left on Via del Pellegrino and then right on Via dei Cartari to reach Corso Vittorio Emanuele II. Pick up Via dei Filippini to the west of Chiesa Nuova. Turn left on Via dei Banchi Nuovi and then right on Via Banco di Santo Spirito. Cross the Ponte Sant' Angelo. Follow Via della Conciliazione west to St. Peter's.

0 ⊢———————⊣ 1 km

Basilica di San Pietro | Castel Sant' Angelo

Musei Capitolini

Chiesa Nuova

Piazza Venezia

Campo de' Fiori

Piazza del Campidoglio

Piazza Trilussa

Foro Romano

Piazza Santa Maria in Trastevere

Piazza Bocca della Verità

Santa Cecilia in Trastevere

Santa Maria in Cosmedin

Isola Tiberina | Teatro di Marcello

A CIRCULAR WALK FROM PIAZZA NAVONA
THROUGH THE HEART OF THE MEDIEVAL CITY

Leave Piazza Navona via the alley in the southeast corner, cross Corso del Rinascimento and follow Via degli Staderari past Sant' Ivo (inside Palazzo di Sapienza) and Sant' Eustachio. Take Via Santa Chiara to Piazza della Minerva and then Via Minerva north to Piazza della Rotonda.

Go east on Via del Seminario then turn right on Via Sant' Ignazio into Piazza Collegio Romano. Cross Via del Corso and wind northeast through Via Santi Apostoli, Via San Marcello and Via dell'Umiltà to emerge south of the Fontana di Trevi. Follow Via del Lavatore, Via delle Scuderie and Via Rasella east to Palazzo Barberini. Walk to Piazza Barberini then take Via Sistina to explore the Spanish Steps. Take Viale Trinità dei Monti to the Pincio Gardens and Villa Borghese.

Drop west to Piazza del Popolo to see Santa Maria del Popolo and go south along Via di Ripetta. From Piazza Porta di Ripetta follow Via Borghese and Via Divino Amore to Piazza Firenze. Continue south to Piazza della Rotonda by way of Piazza in Campo Marzio and Via Maddalena. Take Via Giustiniani west to San Luigi, then follow Via della Scrofa to Sant' Agostino, then return to Piazza Navona.

INFORMATION

Time 4–6 hours
Distance 6km (4 miles; circular tour)
Start/end point ★
Piazza Navona
🚇 el; C5
🚌 40, 46, 62, 64 to Corso Vittorio Emanuele II, or 30, 70, 81, 87, 116, 492 to Corso del Rinascimento
🅲 Start early with Palazzo-Galleria Doria Pamphilj and Palazzo Barberini. Churches at the end of the walk are open late afternoon
🍴 Bar della Pace, Doney, Rosati and Canova (► 70). For ice cream: Tre Scalini and the Gelateria della Palma (► 69)

0   1 km

Pincio | Villa Borghese
Piazza del Popolo
Mausoleo di Augusto
Ara Pacis
Piazza Porta di Ripetta
Sant' Agostino
San Luigi dei Francesi
Piazza Navona
Sant' Ivo
Sant' Eustachio | Piazza della Rotonda
Scalinata della Trinità dei Monti
Piazza Barberini
Palazzo Barberini
Fontana di Trevi
Piazza Collegio Romano

23

Rome by Night

Above: *Cafés in the Campo de' Fiori, a favourite nocturnal meeting place*
Above right: *The dome of St. Peter's silhouetted against the pink glow of evening sky*

NOCTURNAL STROLLS

Rome's trendiest after-dark areas are San Lorenzo, a student and working-class district east of the city, and working-class Testaccio, to the south. Both are some way from the heart of town. So if you don't need to be at the cutting edge, spend the night in Trastevere, an established area full of small squares and pretty streets. To escape its crowds, walk to the Pincio from the top of the Spanish Steps for great sunset views, or wander through the old Ghetto area south of Via delle Botteghe Oscure, beautifully deserted after dark.

After dark the heat of a summer day gives way to balmy evenings and life takes to the streets, allowing you to share in the soft, sweet blandishments of *la dolce vita*, still as vibrant and seductive as in the heady 1950s. Bars and cafés fill with Romans at their sleek and well-dressed best, while Lotharios and pouting, lean-limbed starlets and wannabes glide around the city on snarling Vespas and in open-topped sports cars.

The Pantheon and Colosseum are spectacular under floodlights and romantic under moonlight. St. Peter's takes on a different hue under Rome's velvety night skies—come at midnight or later and you may well have Piazza San Pietro to yourself. The experience is magical.

Much the same can be said of Rome's other great set-pieces, Piazza Navona, the Trevi Fountain and Spanish Steps—although you will not be alone. Piazza Navona, like a great nocturnal salon, fills with street performers, food stalls, artists and locals and visitors there to see and be seen.

If you prefer peace and quiet then walk from one sleepy fountain-splashed piazza to the next, sip an aperitif in a flower-decked terrace or eat under the stars—one of Rome's pleasures. Alternatively, take in an open-air concert in a beautiful Renaissance garden or amid ancient Roman ruins.

ROME's
top 25 sights

The sights are shown on the maps on the inside front cover and inside back cover, numbered **1**–**25** across the city

Basilica di San Pietro

HIGHLIGHTS

- Façade
- Dome
- *Pietà*, Michelangelo
- *Baldacchino,* Bernini
- *St. Peter*, Arnolfo di Cambio
- Tomb of Paul III, Guglielmo della Porta
- Tomb of Urban VIII, Bernini
- Monument to Alexander VII, Bernini

INFORMATION

- ✚ C6; Locator map A2
- ✉ Piazza San Pietro, Città del Vaticano
- ☎ 06 6988 1662/3462
- ◷ Basilica daily 7–7, mid-Mar to Oct; 7–6, rest of year. Dome daily 8–6, mid-Mar to Oct; 8–4, rest of year. Grottos daily 7–6, Apr–Sep; 7–5, rest of year. Treasury daily 9–5.30, Apr–Sep; 9–4, rest of year
- 🍴 Shop
- Ⓜ Ottaviano
- 🚌 64 to Porta Cavalleggeri or 23, 32, 49, 81, 492, 990 to Piazza del Risorgimento
- ♿ Wheelchair access
- 🎟 Basilica free. Dome and Treasury moderate. Grottos expensive

Although the works of art in St. Peter's are rather disappointing, the interior impresses as the spiritual capital of Roman Catholicism with an overwhelming sense of scale and decorative splendour.

The creators The first St. Peter's was built by Constantine around AD326, reputedly on the site where St. Peter was buried following his crucifixion in AD64. Between 1506 and 1626, it was virtually rebuilt to plans by Bramante, and then to designs by Antonio da Sangallo, Giacomo della Porta, Michelangelo and Carlo Maderno. Michelangelo was also responsible for much of the dome, and Bernini finished the façade and the interior.

Baldacchino *and dome*

What to see Michelangelo's unforgettable *Pietà* (1499), behind glass following an attack in 1972, is in the first chapel of the right nave. At the end of the same nave stands a statue of St. Peter: His right foot has been caressed by millions since 1857 when Pius IX granted a 50-day indulgence to anyone kissing it after confession. Bernini's high altar canopy, or *baldacchino* (1624–33), was built during the papacy of Urban VIII, a scion of the Barberini family; it is decorated with bees, the Barberini's dynastic symbol. To its rear are Guglielmo della Porta's Tomb of Paul III (left) and Bernini's influential Tomb of Urban VIII (right). Rome seen from the dome (entrance at the end of the right nave) is *the* highlight of a visit.

Musei Vaticani

The Vatican Museums make up the world's largest museum complex. The 1,400 rooms abound in riches: Greek, Roman and Etruscan sculptures, Renaissance paintings, books, maps, tapestries and frescos.

Treasures of 12 museums Instead of the two days (and 7km/4 miles of walking) needed to do justice to the Vatican Museums, you can follow one of the colour-coded walks, designed to ease your way through the crowds and match the time you have available. Or you might decide on your own priorities, choosing between the collections according to your interest: Egyptian and Assyrian art (the Museo Gregoriano Egizio); Etruscan artefacts (Museo Gregoriano-Etrusco); the more esoteric anthropological collections (Museo Missionario Etnologico); or modern religious art (Collezione d'Arte Religiosa Moderna).

Celebrated works of art Whatever your priorities, several sights should not be missed. Most obvious are the Sistine Chapel (► 28), with Michelangelo's *Last Judgment*, and the four rooms of the Stanze di Raffaello, each of which is decorated with frescos by Raphael. Further fresco cycles by Pinturicchio and Fra Angelico adorn the Borgia Apartment and Chapel of Nicholas V, and are complemented by an almost unmatched collection of paintings in the Vatican Art Gallery (or Pinacoteca). The best of the Greek and Roman sculpture is the breathtaking Laocoön group in the Cortile Ottagono of the Museo Pio-Clementino. The list of artists whose work is shown in the Collezione di Arte Religiosa Moderna is a roll call of the most famous in the last 100 years, from Paul Gauguin and Pablo Picasso to Salvador Dalí and Henry Moore.

HIGHLIGHTS

- Sistine Chapel (► 28)
- Laocoön
- Apollo del Belvedere (Museo Pio-Clementino)
- *Marte di Todi* (Museo Gregoriano-Etrusco)
- Maps Gallery (Galleria delle Carte Geografiche)
- Frescos by Pinturicchio
- Frescos by Fra Angelico
- Stanze di Raffaello
- Pinacoteca
- Room of the Animals (Museo Pio-Clementino)

INFORMATION

- C6; Locator map A2
- Viale Vaticano, Città del Vaticano
- 06 6988 4947/4466/3333
- Mon–Fri 8.45–3.45, Sat and last Sun of month 8.45–1.45, Mar–Oct; Mon–Sat and last Sun of month 8.45–1.45, rest of year. Closed holidays
- Café, restaurant and shop
- Ottaviano
- 23, 32, 49, 81, 492, 990 to Piazza del Risorgimento, 40 to Piazza Pia or 64 to Porta Cavalleggeri
- Wheelchair access
- Very expensive (includes entry to all other Vatican museums); free last Sun of month
- Basilica di San Pietro (► 26), Cappella Sistina (► 28), Castel Sant' Angelo (► 29)

27

Cappella Sistina

HIGHLIGHTS

- Ceiling frescos, Michelangelo
- *Last Judgment*, Michelangelo
- *Baptism of Christ in the Jordan*, Perugino
- Fresco: *Temptation of Christ*, Botticelli
- *Calling of SS. Peter and Andrew*, Ghirlandaio
- *The Delivery of the Keys to St. Peter*, Perugino
- Fresco: *Moses's Journey into Egypt*, Pinturicchio
- *Moses Kills the Egyptian*, Botticelli
- *Last Days of Moses*, Luca Signorelli

INFORMATION

- C6; Locator map A2
- Viale Vaticano, Città del Vaticano
- 06 6988 4947/4466/3333
- Mon–Fri 8.45–3.45, Sat and last Sun of month 8.45–1.45, Mar–Oct; Mon–Sat and last Sun of month 8.45–1.45, rest of year. Closed holidays
- Café, restaurant and shop
- Ottaviano
- 23, 32, 49, 81, 492, 990 to Piazza del Risorgimento
- Wheelchair-accessible routes
- Very expensive (includes entry to all other Vatican museums)

In Michelangelo's frescos the Sistine Chapel has one of the world's supreme masterpieces. Controversially restored between 1980 and 1994, the paintings of this modest-size, hall-like chapel at the heart of the Vatican Museums draw a ceaseless stream of pilgrims.

The chapel The Cappella Sistina (Sistine Chapel) was built by Pope Sixtus IV between 1475 and 1480. The Vatican Palace's principal chapel, it is used by the conclave of cardinals when they assemble to elect a new pope. Decoration of its lower side walls took place between 1481 and 1483, the work, among others, of Perugino, Botticelli, Ghirlandaio, Pinturicchio and Luca Signorelli. From the chapel entrance their 12 paintings compose *Scenes from the Life of Christ* (on the left wall as you face away from the high altar) and *Scenes from the Life of Moses* (on the right wall).

Michelangelo's frescos Pope Julius II commissioned Michelangelo to paint the ceiling in 1508. The frescos, comprising over 300 individual figures, were completed in four years, during which Michelangelo worked in appalling conditions, lying on his back and in extremes of heat and cold. Their narrative describes in nine scenes the story of Genesis and the history of humanity before Christ's coming. In the centre is the *Creation of Adam*. The fresco behind the high altar, the *Last Judgment*, was begun for Pope Paul III in 1534 and completed in 1541. An extraordinary work, it is densely crowded with figures, conveying a powerful sense of movement. It is Michelangelo in a sombre mood, with the righteous rising to paradise accompanied by angels on Christ's right, and the damned drawn irrevocably towards hell on his left.

Castel Sant' Angelo

Castel Sant' Angelo, rising above the river, has served as an army barracks, papal citadel, imperial tomb and medieval prison. Today a 58-room museum here traces the castle's near 2,000-year history, providing a pleasant contrast to the Vatican Museums.

Many incarnations The Castel Sant' Angelo was built by Emperor Hadrian in AD130 as a mausoleum for himself, his family and his dynastic successors. It was crowned by a gilded chariot driven by a statue of Hadrian disguised as the sun god Apollo. Emperors were buried in its vaults until about AD271, when under threat of invasion from Germanic raiders it became a citadel and was incorporated into the city's walls. Its present name arose in AD590, after a vision by Gregory the Great, who while leading a procession through Rome to pray for the end of plague saw an angel sheathing a sword on this spot, an act thought to symbolize the end of the pestilence.

Castle and museum In AD847 Leo IV converted the building into a papal fortress, and in 1277 Nicholas III linked it to the Vatican by a (still visible) passageway, the *passetto*. A prison in the Renaissance, and then an army barracks after 1870, the castle became a museum in 1933. Exhibits, spread over four floors, are scattered around a confusing but fascinating array of rooms and corridors. Best of these is the beautiful Sala Paolina, done with stucco, fresco and *trompe-l'oeil*. The most memorable sight is the 360° view from the castle's terrace, the setting for the last act of Puccini's *Tosca*.

HIGHLIGHTS

- Spiral funerary ramp
- Staircase of Alexander VI
- Armoury
- Hall of Justice
- Fresco: *Justice*, attributed to Domenico Zaga
- Chapel of Leo X: façade by Michelangelo
- Sale di Clemente VII with wall paintings
- Cortile del Pozzo: wellhead
- Prisons (Prigione Storiche)
- Sala Paolina
- View from Loggia of Paul III

INFORMATION

- ✚ F6; Locator map B2
- ✉ Lungotevere Castello 50
- ☎ 06 681 9111
- 🕑 Tue–Sun 9–7/8
- 🍴 Café
- Ⓜ Lepanto
- 🚌 23, 34, 40, 62, 64, 280, 982 to Piazza Cavour or the Lungotevere
- ♿ Poor
- 💰 Expensive
- ↔ Basilica di San Pietro (► 26), Musei Vaticani (► 27), Cappella Sistina (► 28)

A Bernini angel on the Ponte Sant' Angelo

Santa Maria in Trastevere

HIGHLIGHTS

- Romanesque campanile
- Façade mosaics
- Portico
- Ceiling, designed by Domenichino
- Cosmati marble pavement
- Wall tabernacle by Mino del Reame (central nave)
- Byzantine mosaics, upper apse
- Mosaics: *Life of the Virgin* (lower apse)
- *Madonna della Clemenza* in Cappella Altemps
- Cappella Avila: baroque chapel

INFORMATION

- ✚ F11; Locator map B3
- ✉ Piazza Santa Maria in Trastevere
- ☎ 06 581 4802 or 06 581 9443
- ⏲ Daily 7.30–12.30/1, 4–7
- 🚌 H, 8, 630, 780 Viale di Trastevere or 23, 280 to Lungotevere Raffaello Sanzio
- ♿ Wheelchair accessible
- 🖐 Free

One of the most memorable sights of night-time Rome is the 12th-century gold mosaics adorning the façade of Santa Maria in Trastevere, their flood-lit glow casting a gentle light over the milling crowds in the piazza below.

Early church   Santa Maria in Trastevere is among the oldest officially sanctioned places of worship in Rome. It was reputedly founded in AD222, allegedly on the spot where a fountain of olive oil had sprung from the earth on the day of Christ's birth (symbolizing the coming of the grace of God). Much of the present church was built in the 12th century during the reign of Innocent II, a member of the Papareschi, a prominent Trastevere family. Inside, the main colonnade of the nave is composed of reused and ancient Roman columns. The portico, containing fragments of Roman reliefs and inscriptions and medieval remains, was added in 1702 by Carlo Fontana, who was also responsible for the fountain that graces the adjoining piazza.

Mosaics   The façade mosaics probably date from the mid-12th century, and depict the Virgin and Child with ten lamp-carrying companions. Long believed to portray the parable of the Wise and Foolish Virgins, their subject matter is contested, as several 'virgins' appear to be men and only two are carrying unlighted lamps (not the five of the parable). The mosaics of the upper apse inside the church, devoted to the glorification of the Virgin, date from the same period and are Byzantine-influenced works by Greek or Greek-trained craftsmen. Those below, depicting scenes from the life of the Virgin (1291), are by the mosaicist and fresco painter Pietro Cavallini.

Campo de' Fiori

There is nowhere more relaxing in Rome to sit and watch the world go by than Campo de' Fiori, a lovely old piazza whose fruit, vegetable and fish market makes it one of the liveliest and most colourful corners of the old city.

Ancient square   Campo de' Fiori—the 'Field of Flowers'—was turned in the Middle Ages from a meadow facing the ancient Theatre of Pompey (55BC; now Palazzo Pio Righetti) into one of the city's most exclusive residential and business districts. By the 15th century it was surrounded by busy inns and bordellos, some run by the infamous courtesan Vannozza Catanei, mistress of the Borgia pope Alexander VI. By 1600 it had also become a place of execution; Giordano Bruno was burned for heresy on the spot marked by his cowled statue.

Present day   Students, foreigners and tramps mingle with market vendors shouting their wares. Cafés, bars and the wonderfully dingy wine bar at No. 15 have you revelling in street life. One

block south lies Piazza Farnese, dominated by the Palazzo Farnese, a Renaissance masterpiece partly designed by Michelangelo and begun in 1516. It is now home to the French Embassy. One block west is the Palazzo della Cancelleria (1485), once the papal chancellery. The nearby Via Giulia, Via dei

Knife grinder

Baullari, the busy Via dei Cappellari and Via del Pellegrino are all wonderful to explore.

HIGHLIGHTS

- Street market
- Wine bar Vineria Reggio
- Statue of Giordano Bruno
- Palazzo Farnese, Piazza Farnese
- Palazzo della Cancelleria, Piazza della Cancelleria
- Palazzo Pio Righetti
- Via Giulia
- Santa Maria dell'Orazione e Morte: church door decorated in stone skulls
- Via dei Baullari

INFORMATION

- G9; Locator map C3
- Piazza Campo de' Fiori
- Market Mon–Sat 7–1.30
- 40, 46, 62, 64 to Corso Vittorio Emanuele II or H, 46, 62, 64, 70, 87 to Largo di Torre Argentina
- Cobbled streets and some kerbs around piazza
- Free
- Piazza Navona (► 32), Palazzo Spada (► 55), Fontana delle Tartarughe (► 57)

Piazza Navona

HIGHLIGHTS

- Fontana dei Quattro Fiumi
- Fontana del Moro (south)
- Fontana del Nettuno (north)
- Palazzo Pamphilj
- San Luigi dei Francesi (Via Santa Giovanna d' Arco)
- Santa Maria dell'Anima (Via della Pace)

INFORMATION

- ✚ G8; Locator map C2
- ✉ Piazza Navona
- ◎ Spagna
- 🚌 30, 70, 51, 87, 116, 492, 628 to Corso del Rinascimento or 40, 46, 62, 64 to Corso Vittorio Emanuele II
- ♿ Good (Santa Maria della Pace: two steps)

Sant'Agnese in Agone
- ☎ 06 679 4435
- 🕐 Tue–Sat 9–noon, 4–7, Sun 10–1, 4–7

San Luigi dei Francesi
- ☎ 06 6880 3815 or 06 688271
- 🕐 Mon–Wed, Fri–Sun 8–12.30, 3.30–7

Santa Maria della Pace (cloister)
- ☎ 06 686 1156
- 🕐 Mon–Sat 8–noon, 4–7, Sun 10–1

Santa Maria dell'Anima
- ☎ 06 683 3729
- 🕐 Mon–Sat 7.30–7, Sun 8–1, 3–7

Piazza di Spagna may be more elegant and Campo de' Fiori more vivid, but Piazza Navona, with its atmospheric echoes of a 2,000-year history, is a glorious place to amble or stop for a drink at a sun-drenched table.

Shaping history Piazza Navona owes its unmistakable elliptical shape to a stadium and racetrack built here in AD86 by Emperor Domitian. From the Circus Agonalis—the stadium for athletic games—comes the piazza's present name, rendered in medieval Latin as *in agone*, and then in Rome's strangulated dialect as *'n 'agona*. The stadium was used until well into the Middle Ages for festivals and competitions. The square owes its present appearance to its rebuilding by Pope Innocent X in 1644.

Around the piazza Bernini's Fontana dei Quattro Fiumi (1651), the 'Fountain of the Four Rivers' (► 56), dominates. On the west side is the baroque Sant' Agnese (1652–57), its façade designed by Borromini. Beside it stands the Palazzo Pamphilj, commissioned by Innocent X and now the Brazilian Embassy. Further afield, San Luigi dei Francesi is famous for three superlative Caravaggio paintings, and Santa Maria della Pace for a cloister by Bramante and Raphael's frescos of the four *Sybils*.

Fontana dei Quattro Fiumi

Palazzo Altemps

This beautiful building, a stone's throw from Piazza Navona, epitomizes all the best of Renaissance urban architecture, while its series of elegant rooms provides the perfect setting for some of the finest of Rome's classical sculpture.

The building Rome's Museo Nazionale Romano (National Roman Museum) is housed in two superbly restored buildings; the Palazzo Massimo delle Terme, near the station (➤ 54), and here in the Palazzo Altemps, whose odd-sounding name is the Italian corruption of the German name von Hohenemps. Mainly constructed in the 15th century, the building houses a series of charming and intimate rooms, many with vaulted ceilings. One gives access to a splendidly frescoed loggia overlooking the comings and goings of a harmonious inner courtyard. The best time to get a sense of the building's history is when dusk falls, when both the rooms and exhibits are imaginatively lit.

The collections The Palazzo Altemps is home to the famous Ludovisi Collection, amassed by Cardinal Ludovico Ludovisi in the 17th century, as well as the Altemps collection, Egyptian antiques and portraits. Look out downstairs for the *Tiber Apollo*, so called because it was found in the bed of the river in the late 19th century, and the two gigantic statues of Athena. The star of the collection is upstairs, the wonderful *Ludovisi Throne*, a Greek sculpture dedicated as a throne for Aphrodite, the protectress of sailors. Dating from the 5th century BC, the delicate carving portrays the goddess rising from the sea foam, her draperies clinging to her. Finally, do not miss the statue of the *Galatian Soldier and His Wife Committing Suicide*, apparently commissioned by Julius Caesar.

HIGHLIGHTS

- Aphrodite's Throne
- Galatian Soldier statue
- Aula Ottogonale
- Courtyard loggia
- Satyr pouring Wine
- Head of Aphrodite

INFORMATION

- ✚ G7; Locator map C2
- ✉ Piazza Sant' Apollinare 44
- ☎ 06 683 3759
- 🕐 Tue–Sun 9–7.45
- 🚌 30, 70, 81, 87, 116, 492, 628 to Corso Rinascimento
- 🎫 Moderate
- ↔ Pantheon (➤ 35), Piazza Navona (➤ 32)

Santa Maria del Popolo

HIGHLIGHTS

- Cappella Chigi
- *Conversion of St. Paul* and *Crucifixion of St. Peter*, Caravaggio
- *Coronation of the Virgin*, Pinturicchio
- Tombs of Ascanio Sforza and Girolamo Basso della Rovere
- *Nativity*, Pinturicchio
- Fresco: *Life of San Girolamo*, Tiberio d'Assisi
- *Delphic Sybil*, Pinturicchio
- Altar, Andrea Bregno
- Stained glass
- *Assumption of the Virgin*, Annibale Carracci

INFORMATION

- H3; Locator map C1
- Piazza del Popolo 12
- 06 361 0836
- Mon–Sat 7–noon, 4–7, Sun 8–1.30, 4.30–7.30
- Rosati and Canova (➤ 70)
- Flaminio
- 117, 119 to Piazza del Popolo
- Few
- Free
- Villa Giulia (➤ 37), Piazza di Spagna & Spanish Steps (➤ 42), Pincio Gardens (➤ 59), Villa Borghese (➤ 59)

Santa Maria del Popolo's appeal stems from its intimate size and location, and from a wonderfully varied and rich collection of works of art ranging from masterpieces by Caravaggio to some of Rome's earliest stained-glass windows.

Renaissance achievement Founded in 1099 on the site of Nero's grave, Santa Maria del Popolo was rebuilt by Pope Sixtus IV in 1472 and extended later by Bramante and Bernini. The right nave's first chapel, the Cappella della Rovere, is decorated with frescos—*Life of San Girolamo* (1485–90)—by Tiberio d'Assisi, a pupil of Pinturicchio whose *Nativity* (*c*1490) graces the chapel's main altar. A doorway in the right transept leads to the sacristy, noted for its elaborate marble altar (1473) by Andrea Bregno.

Apse The apse contains two fine stained-glass windows (1509) by the French artist Guillaume de Marcillat. On either side are the greatest of the church's monuments: the tombs of the cardinals Ascanio Sforza (1505, left) and Girolamo Basso della Rovere (1507, right). Both are the work of Andrea Sansovino. High on the walls are superb and elegant frescos (1508–10) of the Virgin, Evangelists, the Fathers of the Church and Sybils by Pinturicchio.

North nave The first chapel of the left transept, the Cappella Cerasi, contains three major paintings: the altarpiece, *Assumption of the Virgin*, by Annibale Carracci (above); and Caravaggio's dramatic *Conversion of St. Paul* and the *Crucifixion of St. Peter* (all 1601). The famous Cappella Chigi (1513), the second chapel in the north aisle, was commissioned by the Sienese banker Agostino Chigi, while its architecture, sculpture and paintings are by Raphael.

Pantheon

No other monument suggests the grandeur of ancient Rome as magnificently as this temple whose early conversion to a place of Christian worship has rendered it the most perfect of the city's ancient monuments.

Temple and church   Built by Emperor Hadrian from AD118–28, the Pantheon replaced a temple of 27BC by Marcus Agrippa, son-in-law of Augustus. (Modestly, Hadrian retained the original inscription proclaiming it as Agrippa's work.) It became the church of Santa Maria ad Martyres in AD609 (the bones of martyrs were brought here from the Catacombs) and is now a shrine to Italy's 'immortals', including the artist Raphael and kings Vittore Emanuele II and Umberto I.

An engineering marvel   Massive and simple externally, the Pantheon is even more breathtaking inside, where the scale, harmony and symmetry of the dome in particular are more apparent. The world's largest dome until 1882 (when it was surpassed in the English spa resort of Buxton), it has a diameter of 43.3m (142ft)—equal to its height from the floor. Weight and stresses were reduced by rows of coffers in the ceiling, and the use of progressively lighter materials from the base to the crown. The central oculus, 9m (30ft) in diameter and clearly intended to inspire meditation on the heavens above, lets light (and rain) fall onto the marble pavement far below.

HIGHLIGHTS

- Façade inscription
- The pedimented portico
- Original Roman doors
- Marble interior and pavement
- Coffered dome and oculus
- Tomb of Raphael
- Royal tombs

INFORMATION

- ✚ H8; Locator map C2
- ✉ Piazza della Rotonda
- ☎ 06 6830 0230
- ⏰ Mon–Sat 8.30–7.30, Sun 9–6, public holidays 9–1
- 🚇 Spagna
- 🚌 119 to Piazza della Rotonda or 40, 64, 70, 81 and all other services to Largo di Torre Argentina
- ♿ Good
- 🎟 Free
- ↔ Piazza Navona (► 32), Santa Maria sopra Minerva (► 36)

The Pantheon

Santa Maria sopra Minerva

HIGHLIGHTS

- Egyptian obelisk atop an elephant, Bernini (outside)
- Porch to the Cappella Carafa
- Frescos: *St. Thomas Aquinas* and *The Assumption*, Filippino Lippi, in the Cappella Carafa
- *Risen Christ*, Michelangelo
- Relics of St. Catherine of Siena, and preserved room in sacristy where she died
- Tombs of Clement VII and Leo X, Antonio da Sangallo
- Tomb slab of Fra Angelico
- Tomb of Giovanni Alberini, Mino da Fiesole or Agostino di Duccio
- Monument to Maria Raggi
- Tomb of Francesco Tornabuoni, Mino da Fiesole

INFORMATION

- ✚ H8; Locator map C3
- ✉ Piazza della Minerva 42
- ☎ 06 679 3926
- ⏰ Daily 7–7/7.30
- 🚇 Spagna
- 🚌 H, 8, 30, 40, 46, 62, 64, 70, 81, 87 to Lago di Torre Argentina or 119 to Piazza della Rotonda
- ♿ Stepped access to church
- 🎟 Free

Remarkable in having retained many Gothic features despite Rome's love for the baroque, behind its plain façade Santa Maria sopra Minerva is a cornucopia of tombs, paintings and Renaissance sculpture.

Florentine influences Originally founded in the 8th century over ruins of a temple to Minerva, the church was built in 1280 to a design by two Florentine Dominican monks who modelled it on their own church, Santa Maria Novella.

Inside The interior of the church abounds with beautiful works such as the Cappella Carafa (whose fine porch is attributed to Giuliano da Maiano),

Elephant supporting an obelisk, by Bernini

and Michelangelo's calm statue *The Risen Christ* (1521), left of the high altar. Filippino Lippi painted the celebrated frescos *St. Thomas Aquinas* and the *Assumption* (1488–93). Among other sculptures are the tombs of Francesco Tornabuoni (1480) and that of Giovanni Alberini, the latter decorated with reliefs of Hercules (15th century). Both are attributed to Mino da Fiesole. Other works include Fra Angelico's tomb slab (1455); the tombs of Medici popes Clement VII and Leo X (1536) by Antonio da Sangallo the Younger; and Bernini's monument to Maria Raggi (1643). St. Catherine of Siena, one of Italy's patron saints, is buried beneath the high altar.

Villa Giulia

The Museo Nazionale Etrusca di Villa Giulia houses the world's greatest collection of Etruscan art and artefacts. The exhibits are not always perfectly presented, but it is a revelation to discover this mysterious civilization.

The villa   Built in 1550–55 as a country house and garden for the hedonistic Pope Julius III, the Villa Giulia was designed by some of the leading architects of the day, including Michelangelo and Georgio Vasari. Restoration has rescued the frescoed loggia and the Nymphaeum, a sunken court in the gardens by the Mannerist architect Giacomo da Vignola.

The collection   The exhibits, which range over two floors and 34 rooms, are generally divided between finds from Etruscan sites in northern Etruria (western central Italy, including Vulci, Veio, Cerveteri and Tarquinia) and from excavations in the south (Nemi and Praeneste), including artefacts made by the Greeks. Most notable are the Castellani exhibits, which include vases, cups and ewers, and jewellery from the Minoan period (the latter collection is one of the villa's special treasures). To see the most striking works of art, be selective. Pick through the numerous vases noting the *Tomba del Guerriero* and the *Cratere a Volute*. Note also the *Sarcofago degli Sposi*, a 6th-century BC sarcophagus with figures of a married couple reclining together on a banqueting couch; the engraved marriage coffer known as the *Cista Ficoroni* (4th century BC); the giant terracotta figures, *Hercules and Apollo*; the temple sculptures from Falerii Veteres; and the valuable 7th-century BC relics in gold, silver, bronze and ivory from the Barberini and Bernardini tombs in Praeneste, 39km (24 miles) east of Rome.

HIGHLIGHTS

- *Lamine d'Oro*, Sala di Pyrgi: a gold tablet (left of entrance)
- Vase: *Tomba del Guerriero*
- Terracottas: *Hercules and Apollo*
- *Sarcofago degli Sposi*
- Castellani Collection
- Vase: *Cratere a Volute*
- Finds from Falerii Veteres
- Tomb relics: Barberini and Bernardini
- Marriage coffer: *Cista Ficoroni*
- Gardens with Nymphaeum and reconstructed 'Temple of Alatri'

INFORMATION

- Off map N11; Locator map C1
- Piazzale di Villa Giulia 9
- 06 322 6571
- Tue–Sun 8.30am–7.30pm
- Café and shop
- Flaminio
- 3 or 19 to Viale delle Belle Arti
- Good
- Moderate
- Santa Maria del Popolo (► 34), Galleria Borghese (► 47)

Palazzo-Galleria Doria Pamphilj

HIGHLIGHTS

- *Religion Succoured by Spain* (labelled 10) and *Salome* (29), Titian
- *Portrait of Two Venetians* (23), Raphael
- *Maddalena* (40) and *Rest on the Flight into Egypt* (42), Caravaggio
- *Birth* and *Marriage of the Virgin* (174/176), Giovanni di Paolo
- *Nativity* (200), Parmigianino
- *Innocent X*, Velázquez
- *Innocent X*, Bernini
- *Battle of the Bay of Naples* (317), Pieter Brueghel the Elder
- Salone Verde
- Saletta Gialla

INFORMATION

The Palazzo Doria Pamphilj is among the largest of Rome's palaces. It contains one of the city's finest patrician art collections and offers the chance to admire some of the sumptuously done rooms of its private apartments.

A dynasty Little in the bland exterior of the Palazzo Doria Pamphilj prepares you for the splendour of the beautiful rooms that lie within. The core of the building, which was built over the foundations of a storehouse dating back to ancient times, was erected in 1435, and it has withstood countless alterations and owners. The Doria Pamphilj dynasty was formed by yoking together the Doria, a famous Genoese seafaring clan, and the Pamphilj, a Rome-based patrician family. Most people come here for the paintings, but—when open—you can enjoy a guided tour around some of the private apartments in the 1,000-room palace. The most impressive is the Saletta Gialla (Yellow Room), decorated with 12 Gobelin tapestries made for Louis XV. In the Salone Verde (Green Room) are three important paintings: *Annunciation* by Filippo Lippi, *Portrait of a Gentleman* by Lorenzo Lotto and *Andrea Doria* (a famous admiral) by Sebastiano del Piombo.

Labyrinth of masterpieces The Pamphilj's splendid art collection is displayed in ranks in four broad galleries. Because the works are numbered, not labelled, it's worthwhile to invest in a catalogue from the ticket office. The finest painting by far is the famous Velázquez portrait, *Innocent X* (1650), a likeness that captured the pope's weak and suspicious nature so adroitly that Innocent is said to have lamented that it was 'too true, too true'. The nearby bust by Bernini of the same pope is more flattering.

Musei Capitolini

Few in number, but outstanding, the Greek and Roman sculptures in the Capitoline Museums (Palazzo Nuovo and Palazzo dei Conservatori) make a far more accessible introduction to the subject than the Vatican Museums.

Palazzo Nuovo The Capitoline Museums occupy two palaces on opposite sides of the Piazza del Campidoglio and are linked by an underground passage. Both have recently been restored. Designed by Michelangelo, the Palazzo Nuovo (on the north side) contains most of the finest pieces, none greater than the magnificent 2nd-century AD bronze equestrian statue of Marcus Aurelius (just off the main courtyard). Moved here from outside San Giovanni in Laterano in the Middle Ages, it is now restored and covered. Among the sculptures inside are celebrated Roman copies in marble of Greek originals, including the *Dying Gaul*, *Wounded Amazon*, *Capitoline Venus* and the discus thrower *Discobolus* (▶ 54). In the Sala degli Imperatori is a portrait gallery of busts of Roman emperors.

Palazzo dei Conservatori This former seat of Rome's medieval magistrates contains an art gallery (the Pinacoteca Capitolina) and a further rich hoard of classical sculpture. Bronzes include the 1st-century BC *Spinario*, a boy removing a thorn from his foot, and the 5th-century BC Etruscan *Lupa Capitolina*, the famous she-wolf suckling Romulus and Remus (the twins were added by Antonio Pollaiuolo in 1510). Paintings include works by Caravaggio, Velázquez, Titian, Veronese and Van Dyck.

HIGHLIGHTS

Palazzo Nuovo
- Statue of Marcus Aurelius
- Sculpture: *Capitoline Venus*
- Sculpture: *Dying Gaul*
- Sculpture: *Wounded Amazon*
- Sculpture: *Discobolus*
- Sala degli Imperatori

Palazzo dei Conservatori
- *St. John the Baptist*, Caravaggio
- Bronze: *Lupa Capitolina*
- Bronze: *Spinario*
- Marble figure: *Esquiline Venus*

INFORMATION

- ✚ K9; D6; Locator map D3
- ✉ Musei Capitolini (Capitoline Museums), Piazza del Campidoglio 1
- ☎ 06 574 8042 or 06 574 8030; www.museicapitolini.org
- 🕐 Tue–Sun 9–8
- 🚌 40, 44, 64 and all other services to Piazza Venezia
- ♿ Poor: steps to Piazza del Campidoglio
- 💰 Expensive (free last Sun of month)

Constantine, Palazzo dei Conservatori

39

Santa Maria in Aracoeli

HIGHLIGHTS

- Aracoeli staircase
- Wooden ceiling
- Cosmati pavement
- Nave columns
- Tomb of Cardinal d'Albret, Andrea Bregno
- Tomb of Giovanni Crivelli, Donatello
- Frescos: *Life of St. Bernardino of Siena*
- Tomb of Luca Savelli, attributed to Arnolfo di Cambio
- Tomb of Filippo Della Valle, attributed to Andrea Briosco
- Fresco: *St. Anthony of Padua*, Benozzo Gozzoli

INFORMATION

- ✚ K9; Locator map D3
- ✉ Piazza d'Aracoeli
- ☎ 06 679 8155
- ⊘ Daily 9–12.30, 2.30–5.30
- 🚌 40, 44, 46, 62, 64, 70, 80, 81 and all other services to Piazza Venezia
- ♿ Poor: steep steps to main entrance or steps to Piazza del Campidoglio
- 🎟 Free
- ↔ Palazzo-Galleria Doria Pamphilj (➤ 38), Musei Capitolini (➤ 39), Foro Romano (➤ 43)

Perched atop the Capitoline Hill—long one of Rome's most sacred spots—Santa Maria in Aracoeli, with its glorious ceiling, fine frescos and soft chandelier-lit interior, is a calm retreat from the ferocious traffic and hurrying crowds of Piazza Venezia.

Approach The flight of 124 steep steps approaching Santa Maria was built in 1348 to celebrate either the end of a plague epidemic or the Holy Year proclaimed for 1350. A more convenient entrance is located off the rear left side of the Piazza del Campidoglio. The church is first recorded in AD574, but even then it was old. Emperor Augustus raised an altar here, the Ara Coeli (the Altar of Heaven), with the inscription now on the church's triumphal arch: *Ecce ara primogeniti Dei* (Behold the altar of the firstborn of God). Most of the present structure dates from 1260.

Grandeur Although only one work of art stands out (Pinturicchio's frescos, the *Life of St. Bernardino of Siena*, 1486), there is an overall

sense of grandeur, achieved by virtue of the gilded ceiling (1572–75) celebrating a naval victory over the Turks in 1571, and by the enormous columns in the nave. Tombs to see include those of Cardinal d'Albret, Giovanni Crivelli, Filippo Della Valle and Luca Savelli.

Detail from the Life of St. Bernardino of Siena

Fontana di Trevi

There is no lovelier surprise in Rome than that which suddenly confronts you as you emerge from the tight warren of streets around the Fontana di Trevi, the city's most famous fountain—a sight 'silvery to the eye and ear', in the words of Charles Dickens.

Virgin discovery In its earliest guise the Fontana di Trevi lay at the end of the Aqua Virgo, or Acqua Vergine, an aqueduct built by Agrippa in 19BC (supposedly filled with Rome's sweetest waters). The spring that fed it was reputedly discovered by a virgin, hence its name. (She is said to have shown her discovery to some Roman soldiers, a scene—along with Agrippa's approval of the aqueduct's plans—described in bas-reliefs on the fountain's second tier.) The fountain's liveliness and charm is embodied in the pose of *Oceanus*, the central figure, and the two giant tritons and their horses (symbolizing a calm and a stormy sea) drawing his chariot. Other statues represent Abundance and Health and, above, the Four Seasons, which each carry gifts.

The fountains A new fountain was built in 1453, ordered by Pope Nicholas V who paid for it by taxing wine—Romans sneered that he 'took our wine to give us water'. Its name came from the three roads (*tre vie*) that converged on the piazza. The present fountain was commissioned by Pope Clement XII in 1732 and finished in 1762: Its design was inspired by the Arch of Constantine and is attributed to Nicola Salvi, with possible contributions from Bernini (though the most audacious touch, which combines a fountain with a palace-like façade, was probably by Pietro da Cortona). Those wishing to return to Rome toss a coin (preferably over the shoulder) into the fountain. The money goes to the Italian Red Cross.

HIGHLIGHTS

- *Oceanus* (Neptune)
- *Allegory of Health* (right of *Oceanus*)
- *Virgin Indicating the Spring to Soldiers*
- *Allegory of Abundance* (left of *Oceanus*)
- *Agrippa Approving the Design of the Aqueduct*
- *Triton with Horse* (on the right, symbolizing the ocean in repose)
- *Triton with Horse* (on the left, symbolizing a tempestuous sea)
- Façade of Santi Vincenzo e Anastasio
- Baroque interior of Santa Maria in Trivio

INFORMATION

- K7; D5; Locator map D2
- Piazza Fontana di Trevi
- Always open
- Spagna or Barberini
- 52, 53, 61, 62, 71, 81, 95, 117, 119 and other routes to Via del Corso and Via del Tritone
- Access via cobbled street
- Free
- Pantheon (➤ 35), Santa Maria sopra Minerva (➤ 36), Palazzo-Galleria Doria Pamphilj (➤ 38), Piazza di Spagna & Spanish Steps (➤ 42)

Piazza di Spagna & Spanish Steps

INFORMATION

✚ K5; Locator map C2

✉ Piazza di Spagna

☎ Museo Keats–Shelley 06 678 4235; www.keats-shelley-house.org. Babington's Tea Rooms 06 678 6027. Caffè Greco 06 679 1700. Villa Medici 06 679 8381

🕙 Spanish Steps always open. Museo Keats–Shelley Mon–Fri 9–1, 3–6, Sat 11–2, 3–6. Trinità dei Monti daily 10–12.30, 4–6. Villa Medici occasionally open for exhibitions.

🍴 Caffè Greco, Babington's Tea Rooms (► 71)

🚇 Spagna

🚌 119 to Piazza di Spagna

♿ None for the Spanish Steps

💷 Free except to Museo Keats–Shelley (moderate)

🔁 Santa Maria del Popolo (► 34), Palazzo Barberini (► 44)

Neither old nor particularly striking, the Spanish Steps are nonetheless one of Rome's most famous sights, thanks largely to their popularity as a meeting point, to their views and to their position at the heart of the city's most exclusive shopping district.

Spanish Steps Despite their name, the Spanish Steps were commissioned by the French ambassador, Étienne Gueffier, who in 1723 sought to link Piazza di Spagna with the French-owned church of Trinità dei Monti on the hill above. A century earlier the piazza had housed the headquarters of the Spanish ambassador to the Holy See, hence the name of both the steps and the square.

Around the steps At the base of the steps is the Fontana della Barcaccia, commissioned in 1627 by Urban VIII and designed either by Gian Lorenzo Bernini or by his less famous father, Pietro. The eccentric design represents a half-sunken boat (► 56). As you face the steps from below, to your right stands the Museo Keats–Shelley (► 54), a fascinating collection of literary memorabilia and a working library housed in the lodgings where the poet John Keats died in 1821. To the left are the famed Babington's Tea Rooms (► 71) and to the south the Via Condotti, Rome's most exclusive shopping street. At the top of the steps you can enjoy views past Palazzo Barberini and towards the Quirinal Hill; walk into the simple Trinità dei Monti, with its outside double stairs by Domenico Fontana; and visit the beautiful gardens of the 16th-century Villa Medici (generally open Sunday morning only), the seat of the French Academy in Rome, where scholars study painting, sculpture, architecture, engraving and music.

Foro Romano

The civic and political heart of the Roman Empire was Rome's Forum. Its ruins can be difficult to decipher, but the site is one of the most evocative in the city, the standing stones and fragments conjuring up echoes of a once powerful state.

History The Forum (Foro Romano) started life as a marsh between the Palatine and Capitoline hills, taking its name from a word meaning 'outside the walls'. Later it became a rubbish dump, and, having been drained, a marketplace and a religious shrine. In time it acquired all the structures of Rome's burgeoning civic, social and political life. Over the centuries consuls, emperors and senators embellished it with magnificent temples, courts and basilicas.

Forum and Palatine Two millennia of plunder and decay have left a mish-mash of odd pillars and jumbled stones, which nonetheless can begin to make vivid sense given a plan and some imagination. This strange, empty space is romantic, especially on the Palatine Hill to the south, once covered by a palace. Today orange trees, oleanders and cypresses line the paths, and grasses and wildflowers flourish among the ancient remains. Worth a visit are the Temple of Antoninus and Faustina, the Colonna di Foca, the Curia, the restored Arch of Septimius Severus, the Portico of the Dei Consentes, the Temple of Saturn, Santa Maria Antiqua (the Forum's oldest church), the aisle of the Basilica of the Emperor Maxentius, the House of the Vestal Virgins and the Arch of Titus.

HIGHLIGHTS

- Temple of Antoninus and Faustina (AD141)
- Colonna di Foca (AD608)
- Arch of Septimius Severus (AD203)
- Curia (Senate House, 80BC)
- 12 columns from the Portico of the Dei Consentes (AD367)
- 8 columns from the Temple of Saturn (Tempio di Saturno, 42BC, AD284)
- House of the Vestal Virgins

INFORMATION

- L10; Locator map D3
- Entrances alongside Arco di Settimio Sevoro, near Arco di Tito and Largo Romolo e Remo on Via dei Fori Imperiali
- 06 699 0110 or 06 3996 7700
- Daily 9 to 1 hour before dusk
- Colosseo
- 60, 75, 85, 87, 117, 810, 850 to Via dei Fori Imperiali
- Access difficult to much of site
- Forum free. Palatine expensive (joint ticket with Colosseo)
- Musei Capitolini (➤ 39)

Pillar and capital from the Forum

Palazzo Barberini

The magnificent Palazzo Barberini— designed by Bernini, Borromini and Carlo Maderno—houses a stupendous ceiling fresco and one of Rome's finest art collections, the Galleria Nazionale d'Arte Antica.

Urban's splendour The palace was commissioned by Maffeo Barberini for his family when he became Pope Urban VIII in 1623. The epitome of Rome's high baroque style, it is a maze of suites, apartments and staircases, many still swathed in their sumptuous original decoration. Overshadowing all is the Gran Salone, dominated by Pietro da Cortona's rich ceiling frescos, glorifying Urban as an agent of Divine Providence. The central windows and oval spiral staircase (Scala Elicoidale) are the work of Borromini.

The collection '*Antica*' here means old rather than ancient. Probably the most popular painting in the collection is Raphael's *La Fornarina* (also attributed to Giulio Romano). It is reputedly

Raphael's La Fornarina

a portrait of one of the artist's several mistresses, identified later as the daughter of a *fornaio* (baker). It was executed in the year of the painter's death, a demise brought on, it is said, by his mistress's unrelenting passion. Elsewhere, eminent Italian works from Filippo Lippi, Andrea del Sarto, Caravaggio and Guido Reni stand alongside paintings by leading foreign artists.

Colosseo

The Pantheon may be better preserved and the Forum more historically important, but no other monument in Rome rivals the majesty of the Colosseum, the world's largest surviving structure from Roman antiquity.

Awe-inspring The Colosseum was begun by Emperor Vespasian in AD72 and inaugurated by his son, Titus, in AD80 with a gala that saw 5,000 animals slaughtered in a day (and 100 days of continuous games thereafter). Finishing touches to the 55,000-seat stadium were added by Domitian (AD81–96). Three types of columns support the arcades, and the walls are made of brick and volcanic tufa faced with marble blocks, which were once bound together by metal clamps (removed in AD664). Its long decline began in the Middle Ages, with the pillaging of stone to build churches and palaces. The desecration ended in 1744, when the structure was consecrated in memory of the Christians supposedly martyred in the arena (later research suggests they weren't). Clearing of the site and excavations began late in the 19th century and restoration was carried out in the 20th.

Games Armed combat at the Colosseum went on for some 500 years. Criminals, slaves and gladiators fought each other or wild animals, often to the death. Women and dwarfs also wrestled, and mock sea battles were waged (the arena could be flooded via underground pipes). Spectators exercised the power of life and death over defeated combatants, by waving handkerchiefs to show mercy or by displaying a down-turned thumb to demand the finishing stroke. Survivors' throats were often cut anyway, and the dead were poked with a red-hot iron to make sure they had actually expired.

HIGHLIGHTS

- Circumference walls
- Arches: 80 lower arches for the easy admission of crowds
- Doric columns: lowest arcade
- Ionic columns: central arcade
- Corinthian columns: upper arcade
- Underground cells for animals
- Sockets that once housed binding metal clamps
- *Vomitoria:* interior exits and entrances
- Views from the upper levels

INFORMATION

- M10; Locator map D3
- Piazza del Colosseo, Via dei Fori Imperiali
- 06 700 4261
- Daily 9–7.30, May–Sep; 9–6.30, Apr and Oct; 9–4.30, rest of year. Last admission one hour before closing
- Colosseo
- 60, 75, 81, 85, 87, 117, 175 to Piazza del Colosseo
- Poor to the interior; limited access from Via Celio Vibenna entrance
- Expensive (joint ticket with Palatino)
- Musei Capitolini (► 39), Foro Romano (► 43), San Pietro in Vincoli (► 46)

45

San Pietro in Vincoli

HIGHLIGHTS

- *Moses*, Michelangelo
- Profile self-portrait in the upper part of Moses' beard
- Chains of St. Peter
- Early Christian carved sarcophagus (crypt)
- Mosaic: *St. Sebastian*
- Tomb of Niccolò da Cusa
- *Santa Margherita*, Guercino
- Tomb of Antonio and Piero Pollaiuolo
- Torre dei Margani (Piazza San Pietro in Vincoli), once believed to have been owned by the Borgias

INFORMATION

- M9; Locator map D3
- Piazza di San Pietro in Vincoli 4a
- 06 488 2865
- Mon–Sat 7–12.30, 3.30–7, Sun 8.45–11.30am, Apr–Sep; Mon–Sat 7–12.30, 3.30–6, Sun 8.45–11.30am, rest of year
- Colosseo or Cavour
- 75, 84 to Via Cavour or 60, 75, 81, 85, 87, 117, 175 to Piazza del Colosseo
- Good
- Free
- Foro Romano (➤ 43), Colosseo (➤ 45), Santa Maria Maggiore (➤ 49)

Hidden in a narrow back street, San Pietro in Vincoli is a thoroughly appealing church. Drop by to admire Michelangelo's statue of Moses, one of the most powerful of all the artist's monumental sculptures.

Chains San Pietro in Vincoli takes its name from the chains (*vincoli*) proudly kept in the coffer with bronze doors under the high altar. According to tradition they are the chains used to bind St. Peter while he was held captive in the Mamertine prison (remnants of which are preserved under the church of San Giuseppe near the Forum). Some of the chains found their way to Constantinople, while the rest were housed in San Pietro by Pope Leo I (who had the church specially reconstructed from a 4th-century building for the purpose). When the chains were eventually reunited, they are said to have miraculously fused together. The church has often been transformed and restored. The 20 columns of its interior arcade came from a Roman temple.

Works of art Michelangelo's majestic sculpture (of a patriarchal Moses receiving the Tablets of Stone) was originally designed as part of a 42-figure ensemble for the tomb of Julius II. Michelangelo spent years scouring the Carrara mountains for suitable pieces of stone, but the project never came close to completion, and he described the work as 'this tragedy of a tomb'. Instead, much of his time was spent (reluctantly) on the Sistine Chapel. Also make sure you see the Byzantine mosaic *St. Sebastian* (*c*680), the monument to the Pollaiuolo brothers (*c*1498) by Luigi Capponi and the tomb of Cardinal da Cusa (1464), attributed to the Lombard sculptor Andrea Bregno.

Galleria Borghese

The Galleria Borghese may be small, but what it lacks in quantity it makes up for in quality. It combines paintings and sculptures, including many masterpieces by Gian Lorenzo Bernini, Raphael, Caravaggio and others.

Seductress The Villa Borghese was designed in 1613 as a summer retreat for Cardinal Scipione Borghese, nephew of Pope Paul V, who accumulated most of the collection (acquired by the state in 1902). Scipione was an enthusiastic patron of Bernini, whose works dominate the gallery. The museum's foremost masterpiece is Antonio Canova's *Paolina Borghese* (1804), Napoleon's sister and wife of Camillo Borghese. Depicted bare-breasted, with a come-hither hauteur, Paolina was just as seductive in life. Her jewels, clothes, lovers and the servants she used as footstools all excited gossip.

Temple of Aesculapius, Villa Borghese

Bernini His *David* (1623–24) is said to be a self-portrait, while *Apollo and Daphne* (1622–25), in the next room, is considered his masterpiece. Other Bernini works include the *Rape of Proserpine* (1622) and *Truth Unveiled by Time* (1652).

The paintings Foremost in this wonderful collection are works by Raphael (*The Deposition of Christ*, 1507), Titian (*Sacred and Profane Love*, 1512), Caravaggio (*Boy with a Fruit Basket* and *Madonna dei Palafrenieri*, 1605) and Correggio (*Danae*, 1530).

HIGHLIGHTS

Galleria Borghese
- *Paolina Borghese*, Canova
- *David*, Bernini
- *Apollo and Daphne*, Bernini
- *Madonna dei Palafrenieri*, Caravaggio
- *Sacred and Profane Love*, Titian
- *Deposition of Christ*, Raphael

INFORMATION

Galleria Borghese
- ✚ M3; Locator map D1
- ✉ Piazzale Scipione Borghese 5
- ☎ 06 841 7645; www.galleriaborghese.it Reservations 06 328 101; www.ticketeria.it
- ◷ Tue–Sun 9–7 (reservations obligatory). Closed public holidays
- Ⓜ Spagna or Flaminio
- 🚌 116 to Viale del Museo Borghese, or 52, 53, 910 to Via Pinciana or 3, 19 to Via delle Belle Arti
- ♿ Steps to front entrance
- Moderate
- ↔ Villa Giulia (➤ 37), Piazza di Spagna & Spanish Steps (➤ 42), Palazzo Barberini (➤ 44)

San Clemente

HIGHLIGHTS

- Choir screen
- Chapel of St. Catherine: fresco cycle
- Ciborio: altar canopy
- Apse mosaic: *The Triumph of the Cross*
- Monument to Cardinal Roverella, Giovanni Dalmata (upper church)
- Fresco: *Miracle of San Clemente*
- Fresco: *Legend of Sisinnio*
- Triclinium
- Altar of Mithras: bas-relief of Mithras slaying the bull

No site in Rome reveals as vividly the layers of history that underpin the city as this beautiful medieval ensemble built over a superbly preserved 4th-century church and the remains of a 3rd-century Mithraic temple.

Upper church The present San Clemente—named after Rome's fourth pope—was built between 1108 and 1184 to replace an earlier one that was sacked by the Normans in 1084. Almost untouched since, its medieval interior is dominated by the 12th-century marble panels of the choir screen and pulpits and the glittering 12th-century apse mosaic, *The Triumph of the Cross*. Equally captivating are the *Life of St. Catherine* frescos (1428–31) by Masolino da Panicale.

Mithraic temple

Below ground Steps descend to the lower church, which retains traces of 8th- to 11th-century frescos of San Clemente and the legends of Sts. Alessio and Sisinnio. More steps lead deeper into the twilight world of the best-preserved of the 12 Mithraic temples uncovered in Rome. (Mithraism was a popular, men-only cult, eclipsed by Christianity.) Here are an altar with a bas-relief of Mithras ritually slaying a bull, and the triclinium, used for banquets and rites. Excavations are revealing parts of the temple, and the 1,900-year-old remains of buildings, streets and an underground stream, which you can hear even today, that may have formed part of ancient Rome's drainage system.

INFORMATION

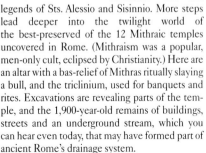

- ✚ N11; Locator map E3
- ✉ Via di San Giovanni in Laterano
- ☎ 06 7045 1018
- 🕐 Mon–Sat 9–12.30, 3–6, Sun 10–12.30, 3–6
- 🚌 60, 76, 81, 85, 87, 117, 175 to Piazza del Colosseo or 85, 117, 850 to Via di San Giovanni in Laterano
- 🎫 Free; excavations inexpensive

Santa Maria Maggiore

Santa Maria Maggiore is Rome's finest Early Christian basilica, thanks to its magnificent mosaic-swathed interior. It is also the only church in the city where mass has been celebrated every single day since the 5th century.

History According to a myth, the Virgin appeared to Pope Liberius on 5 August AD352, and told him to build a church exactly where snow would fall the next day. Although it was summer, snow fell, marking the outlines of a basilica on the Esquiline Hill. Legend aside, the church probably dates from AD430, though the campanile (the tallest in Rome at 75m/246ft) was added in 1377 and the interior and exterior were altered in the 13th and 18th centuries. The coffered ceiling, attributed to Giuliano da Sangallo, was reputedly gilded with the first gold to arrive from the New World, a gift from Spain to Alexander VI (note his Borgia bull emblems).

Rich decoration Beyond the general splendour, the main treasures are the 36 mosaics in the architraves of the nave, 5th-century depictions of the lives of Moses, Abraham, Isaac and Jacob, framed by some 40 ancient columns. Also compelling are the mosaics on the triumphal arch: the *Annunciation* and *Infancy of Christ*. In the 13th-century apse are mosaics by Jacopo Torriti, including the *Coronation of the Virgin* (1295), the pinnacle of Rome's medieval mosaic tradition. Look out, too, for mosaics in the entrance loggia by Filippo Rusuti. Other highlights include the Cappella Sistina (tomb of Pope Sixtus V) by Domenico Fontana, 1588; the Cappella Paolina, built by Paul V (1611); and Giovanni di Cosma's tomb of Cardinal Rodriguez (1299). The high altar reputedly contains a relic of Christ's crib, the object of devotion of countless pilgrims.

HIGHLIGHTS

- Mosaics: upper tier of entrance loggia
- Coffered ceiling
- Mosaic cycle: 36 Old Testament scenes
- Mosaics: triumphal arch
- Apse mosaic: *Coronation of the Virgin*, Jacopo Torriti
- Four reliefs from a papal altar, Mino del Reame
- Fresco fragments: *Prophets*, attributed to Cimabue, Pietro Cavallini or Giotto (apse)
- Cappella Sistina
- Cappella Paolina
- Tomb of Cardinal Rodriguez, Giovanni di Cosma

INFORMATION

- P8; Locator map E3
- Piazza di Santa Maria Maggiore and Piazza dell'Esquilino
- 06 483 195 or 06 581 4802
- Daily 7–7
- Termini or Cavour
- 16, 70, 71, 75, 84, 360 to Piazza di Santa Maria Maggiore
- Poor: access is easiest from Piazza di Santa Maria Maggiore
- Free
- Palazzo Barberini (► 44), San Pietro in Vincoli (► 46)

San Giovanni in Laterano

HIGHLIGHTS

- Central portal: bronze doors
- Fresco: *Boniface VIII*, attributed to Giotto
- Cappella Corsini
- Frescoed tabernacle
- High altar reliquary
- Apse mosaic, Jacopo Torriti
- Cloister: columns and inlaid marble mosaics
- Papal altar: only the pope can celebrate mass here
- Scala Santa
- Baptistery

INFORMATION

- ✚ Off map Q11; Locator map E3
- ✉ Piazza di San Giovanni in Laterano
- ☎ 06 6988 6433
- ◷ Church and cloister daily 7–6.45, Apr–Sep; 7–6, rest of year. Scala Santa daily 6.15–noon, 3–6.30. Baptistery daily 7–12.30, 3.30–7.30
- ⌸ San Giovanni
- ◷ 3, 6, 81, 85, 87, 117, 850 to Piazza di San Giovanni in Laterano
- ♿ Poor: steps to church
- ⏻ Church, Scala Santa, baptistery free. Cloister inexpensive
- ⟳ Colosseo (➤ 45), San Pietro in Vincoli (➤ 46), San Clemente (➤ 48)

San Giovanni's soaring façade can be seen from afar, its distinctive statues rising over the rooftops—a deliberate echo of St. Peter's—reminding us that this is the cathedral church of Rome and the pope's titular see in his role as bishop of Rome.

Early days   A 4th-century palace here provided a meeting place for Pope Miltiades and Constantine (the first Christian emperor), later becoming a focus for Christianity. Earthquakes, fires and Barbarians destroyed the earliest churches on the site, so the façade, modelled on St. Peter's, dates from 1735, and Borromini's interior from 1646. It was the papal residence in Rome until the 14th century, when the popes moved to the Vatican.

Nave with statues of the Apostles

Interior treasures   Bronze doors from the Forum's Curia usher you into the cavernous interior, its chill whites and greys redeemed by a fabulously ornate ceiling. Other highlights include an apse mosaic by Jacopo Torriti (1288–94) and the beautiful cloister (off the north transept). A high altar reliquary is supposed to contain the heads of St. Peter and St. Paul, and a frescoed tabernacle is attributed to Arnolfo di Cambio and Fiorenzo de Lorenzo. Outside are the Scala Santa, reputedly the steps ascended by Christ at his trial in Jerusalem. The octagonal baptistery dates back to the time of Constantine and was the model for many subsequent baptisteries.

ROME's
best

Roman Sites

TRIUMPHAL ARCHES

Two of Rome's greatest contributions to architecture were the basilica and the triumphal arch, the latter raised by the Roman Senate on behalf of a grateful populace to celebrate the achievements of victorious generals and emperors. Returning armies and their leaders passed through the arches, bearing the spoils of war past a cheering crowd. Only three major arches survive in Rome—the Arch of Constantine and, in the Forum, the arches of Titus and Septimius Severus. But the influence of the form continues to be felt in London's Marble Arch and Paris's Arc de Triomphe.

ARCO DI COSTANTINO

Triumphal arches, like celebratory columns, were usually raised as monuments to military achievement, in this case the victory of Emperor Constantine over his imperial rival Maxentius, at the Battle of Ponte Milvio to the north of the city in AD312. It was one of the last great monuments to be built in ancient Rome, and at 21m (69ft) high and 26m (85ft) wide it is also the largest and best-preserved of the city's arches. Most of its reliefs were taken from earlier buildings, partly out of pragmatism and partly out of a desire to link Constantine's glories with those of the past. The battle scenes of the central arch show Trajan at war with the Dacians, while another describes a boar hunt and sacrifice to Apollo, carved in the time of Hadrian (2nd century AD).

➕ M11 ✉ Piazza del Colosseo-Via di San Gregorio, Via dei Fori Imperiali 🕐 Always open 🚇 Colosseo 🚌 60, 75, 81, 85, 87, 117,175 to Piazza del Colosseo 🎫 Free

TERME DI CARACALLA

The Baths of Caracalla were not the largest baths in ancient Rome (those of Diocletian near the present-day Piazza della Repubblica were bigger). But they were the city's most luxurious and could accommodate as many as 1,600 bathers at one time. Started by Septimius Severus in AD206, and completed 11 years later by his son, Caracalla, they were designed as much as a gathering place as for hygiene, complete with gardens, libraries, sports facilities, stadiums, lecture rooms, shops—even hairdressers. They were open to both sexes, but bathing for men and women took place at different times. Something of the Terme's scale can still be gauged from today's ruins, although the site is perhaps now best known as a stage for outdoor opera performed here in the summer.

➕ Off map K11 ✉ Via delle Terme di Caracalla 52 ☎ 06 3996 7700; on-line booking www.pierreci.it 🕐 Tue–Sun 9–1 hour before sunset, Mon 9–2; closed holidays 🚇 Circo Massimo 🚌 60, 75, 81, 175, 673 to Via di San Gregorio-Via delle Terme di Caracalla 🎫 Moderate

Carving from the Terme di Caracalla

CIRCO MASSIMO

This enormous grassy arena follows the outline of a stadium once capable of seating 300,000 people. Created to satisfy the passionate Roman appetite for chariot racing, and the prototype for almost all subsequent racecourses, it was begun around 326BC and modified frequently before the occasion of its last recorded use under Totila the Ostrogoth in AD549. Much of the original structure was robbed of its stone—old monuments were often ransacked for building materials—but the *spina* (the circuit's dividing wall) remains, marked by a row of cypresses, the ruins of the imperial box and the open arena, now a public park. Avoid after dark.

✚ K11 ✉ Via del Circo Massimo 🕓 Always open
🚇 Circo Massimo 🚍 60, 75, 81, 160, 175, 628, 673 to Piazza di Porta Capena 🎫 Free

COLONNA DI MARCO AURELIO

The Column of Marcus Aurelius (AD 180–96) was built to celebrate Aurelius's military triumphs over hostile north European tribes. It is composed of 27 separate drums of Carrara marble welded into a seamless whole, and is done with a continuous spiral of bas-reliefs commemorating episodes from the victorious campaigns. Aurelius is depicted no fewer than 59 times, though curiously never actually in battle. The summit statue is of St. Paul, crafted by Domenico Fontana in 1589 to replace the 60th depiction of Aurelius.

✚ J7 ✉ Piazza Colonna, Via del Corso 🕓 Always open
🚇 Barberini 🚍 62, 63, 81, 85, 95, 117, 119 and all routes to to Via del Corso 🎫 Free

MERCATI DI TRAIANO

Lack of space in the Forum prompted the building of the Imperial Fora (Fori Imperiali). They were begun in the 1st century BC by Julius Caesar and augmented by emperors Augustus, Vespasian, Nerva and Trajan; the ruins of the buildings constructed during their rule lie either side of the Via dei Fori Imperiali. Part of the largest, Trajan's Forum, was the Mercati Traianei, constructed at the beginning of the 2nd century AD as a semicircular range of halls on three levels. Two survive in excellent condition, together with many of the 150 booths that once traded rare and expensive commodities. Look in particular at the Via Biberata, named after *pipera* (pepper).

✚ K9 ✉ Via IV Novembre 94 ☎ 06 679 0048; reservations 06 6978 0532 🕓 Tue–Sun 9–6.30, Apr–Sep; Tue–Sun 9–4:30, rest of year 🚇 Cavour 🚍 H, 40, 60, 64, 70, 117, 170 and other routes to Via IV Novembre 🎫 Free

Museums

MUSEO BARRACCO

This modest collection of Assyrian, Egyptian, Greek, Etruscan and Roman artefacts is housed in the charming Piccola Farnesina, a miniature Renaissance palace.
✚ G8 ✉ Corso Vittorio Emanuele II 166 ☎ 06 6880 6848 🕐 Currently closed for restoration (enquire for reopening date) 🚍 40, 46, 62, 64, 916 and other services to Corso Vittorio Emanuele II 💰 Inexpensive (expensive for special exhibitions)

MUSEO KEATS–SHELLEY

Since 1909 this has been a museum and library for students of the Romantic poets Keats and Shelley, both of whom died in Italy. Books, pictures and essays lie scattered around the 18th-century house.
✚ K5 ✉ Piazza di Spagna ☎ 06 678 4235 🕐 Mon–Fri 9–1, 3–6, Sat 11–2, 3–6 🚇 Spagna 🚍 119 to Piazza di Spagna 💰 Inexpensive

MUSEO NAZIONALE ROMANO–PALAZZO MASSIMO DELLE TERME

One of the two buildings (the other being Palazzo Altemps, ➤ 33) housing Rome's magnificent classical collections, the Palazzo Massimo is an elegant and airy 19th-century palace, beautifully renovated for the millennium. Here you'll find some of Rome's greatest classical treasures, ranging from naked gods and games players to sarcophagi and goddesses. Don't miss the superb portrait busts, the great *Discus Thrower*, or the wonderful Roman frescos and mosaics on the upper floor.
✚ P7 ✉ Piazza dei Cinquecento 67 ☎ Reservations 06 3996 7700; www. pierreci.it 🕐 Tue–Sun 9–7.45 🚇 Repubblica 🚍 All services to Termini and Piazza dei Cinquecento 💰 Moderate (joint pass available with Palazzo Altemps)

MUSEO DEL PALAZZO VENEZIA

Built in 1455 for Pietro Barbo (later Pope Paul II), and one of the city's first Renaissance palaces, the former Venetian Embassy became the property of the state in 1916; Mussolini harangued the crowds from the balconies. Today the museum hosts travelling exhibitions and a fine permanent collection that includes Renaissance paintings, sculpture, armour, ceramics, silverware and objets d'art.
✚ J8 ✉ Palazzo Venezia, Via del Plebiscito 118 ☎ 06 6999 4319 🕐 Tue–Sun 9–2; closed holidays 🚍 All services to Piazza Venezia

The Discus Thrower (Discobolus)

Art Galleries

PALAZZO CORSINI

Though in a separate building, this gallery is part of the Palazzo Barberini's Galleria Nazionale. Originally part of the Corsini family's 17th-century collection, it became state property in 1883. Pictures from the 16th–18th century hang alongside bronzes and sculptures in a series of elegant rooms. Look out for Bassano's touching *Adoration of the Shepherds*, Murillo's gentle *Madonna and Child* and the powerful *St. John the Baptist* by Caravaggio.

➕ F9 ✉ Via della Lungara 10 ☎ 06 6880 2323; reservations 06 328 101; www.ticketeria.it 🕐 Tue–Sun 8.30–7 🚌 23, 116, 280, 870 to Lungotevere Farnesina 💶 Moderate

A ceiling in the Villa Farnesina

PALAZZO SPADA

This pretty palazzo, with a creamy stucco façade (1556–60), contains four rooms where you can admire the 17th–18th-century Spada family paintings. Cardinal Spada is portrayed by Guido Reni; there's a stunning Borromini *Perspective* and works by Albrecht Dürer, Andrea del Sarto and others.

➕ G9 ✉ Piazza Capo di Ferro 3–Vicolo del Polverone 15b ☎ 06 686 1158; reservations 06 328 101, www.ticketeria.it 🕐 Tue–Sat 9–7, Sun 9–1 🚌 H, 8, 63, 630, 780 to Via Arenula 💶 Moderate

PALAZZO-GALLERIA COLONNA

The best painting of this mostly 16th- to 18th-century collection is Annibale Carracci's bucolic scene of a peasant eating beans.

➕ K8 ✉ Via della Pilotta 17 ☎ 06 679 4362 or 06 678 4350 🕐 Sat only 9–1, Sep–Jul 🚌 64, 70, 75, 81, 170 and other routes to Piazza Venezia 💶 Moderate

VILLA FARNESINA

This lovely Renaissance villa was completed in 1511 for Agostino Chigi (➤ panel, right) by Baldassare Peruzzi and later sold to the influential Farnese family. It is best known for the Loggia of Cupid and Psyche, decorated with frescos (1517) by Raphael; for Il Sodoma's masterpiece *Scenes from the Life of Alexander the Great* (1516–17); and for the Salone delle Prospettive, Peruzzi's trompe l'oeil views of Rome.

➕ F9 ✉ Via della Lungara 230 ☎ 06 6880 1767 🕐 Mon–Sat 9–1 🚌 23, 280 to Lungotevere Farnesina 💶 Moderate

AGOSTINO CHIGI

Agostino Chigi (*d* 1512), from Siena, made his banking fortune by securing Rome's prize business–the papal account. He became renowned for flinging the family silver into the Tiber after gargantuan feasts at the Villa Farnesina. This extravagant gesture was not all it seemed, however, for Chigi omitted to tell his admiring diners that a net strung below the water caught the loot for the next banquet.

Fountains

Fontana delle Naiadi

FONTANA DELLE API

Bernini's small but captivating fountain was commissioned in honour of Pope Urban VIII, leading light of the Barberini clan. It depicts a scallop shell, a symbol of life and fertility—a favourite Bernini conceit—at which three bees (*api*), taken from the Barberini coat of arms, have settled to drink.

🛨 L6 ⊠ Piazza Barberini 🚇 Barberini 🚌 52, 53, 61, 62, 80, 95, 116, 119 to Piazza Barberini or Via del Tritone

FONTANA DELLA BARCACCIA

Commissioned by Pope Urban VIII, this eccentric little fountain (1627–29) at the base of the Spanish Steps (► 42) is the work of either Gian Lorenzo Bernini or his father Pietro. It represents a half-sunken ship and, translated literally, its name means Fountain of the Wretched Boat. Bernini was unable to create a greater aquatic display because of the low water pressure in the aqueduct feeding the fountain.

🛨 K5 ⊠ Piazza di Spagna 🚇 Spagna 🚌 119 to Piazza di Spagna

FONTANA DEL MORO

Designed in 1575 by Giacomo della Porta, the fountain at Piazza Navona's southern end shows a North African 'Moor' (actually a marine divinity) grappling with a dolphin, a figure added by Antonio Mori from a design by Bernini.

🛨 G7 ⊠ Piazza Navona 🚌 30, 70, 81, 87, 116, 492, 628 to Corso del Rinascimento or 40, 46, 62, 64 to Corso Vittorio Emanuele II

FONTANA DELLE NAIADI

The 'Fountain of the Naiads' in Piazza della Repubblica, although of little historical interest or artistic value, is probably one of the most erotic works of art on public display anywhere in Italy. Designed by Mario Rutelli, the sculptures were added in 1901. Water plays seductively over four frolicking and suggestively clad bronze nymphs, each entwined in the phallic tentacles of one of four marine creatures. Each beast represents water in one of its forms: The swan signifying lakes, the sea-horse oceans, the water snake rivers and the lizard underground streams.

FONTANA PAOLA

The five arches and six granite columns of the monumental façade fronting this majestic fountain were built between 1610 and 1612 to carry the waters of Trajan's aqueduct, which had been restored by Pope Paul V. The columns were removed from the old St. Peter's, while many of the precious marbles were filched from the Temple of Minerva in the Imperial Fora.

🛨 E11 ⊠ Via Garibaldi 🚌 870 to the Gianicolo

FONTANA DEI QUATTRO FIUMI

Bernini's spirited Fountain of the Four Rivers at the heart of Piazza Navona (► 32) was designed for Pope Innocent X in 1648 as part of a scheme to improve the approach to the Palazzo Doria Pamphilj. It was unveiled in 1651. Its four figures represent the four rivers of Paradise (the Nile, Ganges, Danube and Plate), and the four 'corners' of the world (Africa, Asia, Europe and America). The dove atop the central obelisk is a symbol of the Pamphilj family, of which Innocent was a member.

➕ G7 ✉ Piazza Navona 🚌 30, 70, 81, 87, 116, 492, 628 to Corso del Rinascimento or 40, 46, 62, 64 to Corso Vittorio Emanuele II

FONTANA DELLE TARTARUGHE

This tiny creation (1581–84) is one of Rome's most delightful sights, thanks to the tortoises, probably added by Bernini in 1658 (they are now copies).

➕ H9 ✉ Piazza Mattei 🚌 H, 8, 63, 630, 780 to Via Arenula or 30, 70, 81, 87, 116 and other services to Largo di Torre Argentina

FONTANA DEL TRITONE

Like its companion piece, the Fontana delle Api (➤ 56), the Fountain of Triton (1643) was also designed by Bernini for Urban VIII. One of the sculptor's earliest fountains, the Fontana del Tritone is made of travertine rather than the more usual marble. It depicts four dolphins supporting twin scallop shells bearing the Barberini coat of arms, on which the triumphant Triton is enthroned.

➕ L6 ✉ Piazza Barberini 🚇 Barberini 🚌 52, 53, 61, 62, 80, 95, 116, 119 to Piazza Barberini or Via del Tritone

LE QUATTRO FONTANE

These four linked fountains (1588–93) sit at a busy crossroads close to Via Nazionale. Each contains a reclining deity: The two female figures are probably Juno and Diana; the male figure is the Nile or Aniene; and the last figure, shown with the she-wolf, is a river god representing the Tiber.

➕ M7 ✉ Via delle Quattro Fontane-Via del Quirinale 🚇 Repubblica 🚌 H, 40, 60, 64, 70, 117, 170 to Via Nazionale

ARTISTIC RIVALRY

Well-worn Roman myths surround Bernini's Fontana dei Quattro Fiumi. One suggests the veiled figure of the Nile symbolizes the sculptor's dislike for the church of Sant' Agnese, designed by his fierce rival, Borromini (the veil actually symbolizes the river's unknown source). Another claims the figure representing the Plate is holding up his arm as if in horror of the church (either appalled by its design or afraid it is about to fall down). Neither theory is correct, for Bernini finished the fountain before Borromini had even begun work on his church.

Fontana dei Quattro Fiumi

Parks & Gardens

Via Appia Antica

CIMITERO ACATTOLICO

Described on more than one occasion as the 'most beautiful cemetery in the world', this bucolic cemetery for non-Catholics is also something of a literary shrine (► panel left), owing to the graves of poets such as the young Englishman John Keats, whose tombstone bears the epitaph 'Here lies One whose Name was Writ in Water'. As late as the 19th century, burials here had to take place at night to avoid provoking attacks from outraged Catholics.
➕ Off map K11 ✉ Via Caio Cestio 6, Testaccio ☎ 06 574 1141/1900 🕐 Tue–Sun 9–2 hours before dusk (subject to change without notice) 🚌 3, 23, 30, 60, 75, 118, 280 to Via Marmorata or Piazza di Porta San Paolo 💶 Free (donation expected)

ORTO BOTANICO

Trastevere has few open spaces, so these university gardens and their 7,000 or so botanical species—originally part of the Palazzo Corsini—provide a welcome slice of green shade.
➕ E10 ✉ Largo Cristina di Svezia, off Via Corsini ☎ 06 4991 7107 🕐 Mon–Sat 9–6.30, in summer; otherwise varies. Closed holidays and Aug 🚌 23, 280 to Lungotevere Farnesina 💶 Inexpensive

PALATINO E ORTI FARNESIANI

After a stroll around the Forum it's worth making time to climb the Palatine Hill to enjoy this peaceful spot, designed in the 16th century by the great Renaissance architect Giacomo Vignola. Orange groves, cypresses and endless drowsy corners, all speckled with flowers and ancient stones, make up the Orti Farnesiani, which were laid out over the ruins of the palace that once stood here.
➕ Off map L11 ✉ Entrances from Via di San Gregorio and other entrances to the Roman Forum ☎ 06 3996 7700 🕐 Daily 9–1 hour before dusk 🚇 Colosseo 🚌 75, 84, 87, 117, 175 to Via dei Fori Imperiali 💶 Expensive (joint ticket with Colosseum)

PARCO OPPIO

This relaxing area of park, once part of a palace complex built by Nero and redeveloped by Trajan, rests the eyes and feet after visits to the Colosseum, San Clemente or San Giovanni in Laterano. A community meeting place, it's a welcoming mixture of grass and walkways (and feral cats), complete with promenading mothers, a children's playground and the entrance to Nero's Domus Aurea.
➕ N10 ✉ Via Labicana-Viale del Monte Oppio 🕐 Always open 🚌 3, 85, 87, 810, 850 to Via Labicana 💶 Free

PARCO SAVELLO

Close to Santa Sabina (a pretty church in its own right), the little-known Parco Savello lies closer to the centre than you might expect. Its hilly position provides a lovely panorama over the Tiber and the city beyond.

➕ Off map J11 ✉ Via Santa Sabina, Aventino 🕐 Daily dawn–dusk 🚌 175 💶 Free

PINCIO

The park was laid out in the early 19th century, but the hill site has always been popular: In ancient times the patricians built lavish

Villa Doria Pamphilj

villas and gardens here. Be sure to walk to the Pincio from Piazza del Popolo or Piazza di Spagna to enjoy the wonderful views (best at dusk) across the rooftops to St. Peter's.

➕ J3 ✉ Piazza del Pincio 🕐 Daily dawn–dusk 🚌 95, 117, 119 to Piazzale Flaminio or Piazza del Popolo 💶 Free

VIA APPIA ANTICA

Once an imperial highway, this old roadway so close to the city centre is now an evocative cobbled lane fringed with ancient monuments, tombs, catacombs and lovely open country (► panel).

➕ Off map L11 ✉ Via Appia Antica 🕐 Always open 🚌 118 from Terme di Caracalla or 218 from Piazza San Giovanni in Laterano 💶 Free

VILLA BORGHESE

Rome's largest central park was laid out between 1613 and 1616 as the grounds of the Borghese family's summer villa. Smaller now, and redesigned in the 18th century during the fashion for informal, English-style parks, it still provides a shady retreat. Walkways, woods and lakes are complemented by fountains, a racetrack and children's playgrounds. There is also a zoo, although it is rather tawdry.

➕ K3 ✉ Porta Pinciana-Via Flaminia 🕐 Daily dawn–dusk 🚇 Flaminio 🚌 3, 19, 88, 95, 116, 117, 119, 495 💶 Free

VILLA CELIMONTANA

Set on one of the southern hills of ancient Rome and scattered with the remains of ancient buildings, this is one of Rome's lesser-known parks, easily accessible from the Colosseum and San Giovanni in Laterano.

➕ Off at N11 ✉ Piazza della Navicella 🕐 Daily 7–dusk 🚌 3 to Via dei Parco del Celio or 81, 117 to Via Claudia 💶 Free

VILLA DORIA PAMPHILJ

This huge area of parkland—laid out for Prince Camillo Pamphilj in the mid-17th century—is probably too far from the centre if you are just making a short visit to Rome. If you have time to spare, however, and fancy a good long walk away from the crowds, there is nowhere better.

➕ A11 ✉ Via di San Pancrazio 🕐 Daily dawn–dusk 🚌 44, 75, 870 to the Gianicolo 💶 Free

VIA APPIA ANTICA

The Appian Way was built in 312BC by Appius Claudius Caecus to link Rome with Capua; in 194BC it was extended to Brindisi (520km/322 miles and 13 days' march away). In 71BC it was the spot where 6,000 of Spartacus's troops were crucified during a slaves' revolt; it bore witness to the funeral processions of Sulla (78BC) and Augustus (AD14); it was the road along which St. Paul was marched as prisoner in AD56; and close to the city walls was the point at which St. Peter (fleeing Rome) encountered Christ and, famously, asked him *'Domine, quo vadis?'* ('Lord, where are you going?').

Mosaics

MOSAICS

Mosaics were a major decorative feature of ancient Roman buildings and early medieval Christian churches. Wall paintings were equally popular, but less resilient, which is why so few survive from the Roman period. Some of the best wall decorations of the Classical age can be seen in the Palazzo Massimo (➤ 54). Many Roman techniques and traditions were inherited from the Greeks, and

Santa Prassede ceiling mosaics

over the centuries tastes varied between monochrome backgrounds and simple pattern mosaics to highly coloured and detailed narratives. Christian mosaics in churches initially copied Roman and Greek models, but increasingly adopted the brilliant gold backgrounds used in Byzantine mosaics from the east.

SANT' AGNESE FUORI LE MURA

Compare the outstanding Byzantine 7th-century mosaics in the apse of Sant' Agnese Fuori le Mura (St. Agnes Outside the Walls) with the earlier mosaics in nearby Santa Costanza. The church was built around AD342 by Constantia to be close to the tomb of the martyred Sant' Agnese. Although clumsily restored in 1855, the mosaics have survived intact. They show Agnes, with the sword of her martyrdom at her feet, flanked by the church's 7th-century rebuilder Pope Honorius I.

➕ Q3 ✉ Via Nomentana 349 ☎ 06 861 0840 ⏰ Tue–Sat 9–noon, 4–6, Mon 9–noon 🚌 36, 60, 62, 84, 90 to Via Nomentana-Via di Santa Costanza 💶 Church free; catacombs moderate

SANTA COSTANZA

Exquisite 4th-century mosaics stand out in this church, originally built as a mausoleum for Constantia and Helena, Emperor Constantine's daughters. Note their white background, in contrast to the gold in later Byzantine work, and the pagan icons adapted to Christian use—especially the lamb and peacock, symbols of innocence and immortality respectively.

➕ Q3 ✉ Via Nomentana 349 ☎ 06 861 0840 ⏰ Tue–Sat 9–noon, 4–6, Mon 9–noon 🚌 36, 60, 62, 84, 90 to Via Nomentana-Via di Santa Costanza 💶 Inexpensive

SANTA MARIA IN DOMNICA AND SANTO STEFANO ROTONDO

Like those in Santa Prassede (➤ 61), the glorious mosaics in the apse of the 9th-century Santa Maria in Domnica were commissioned by Pope Paschal I, depicted at the foot of the Virgin and Child (his square halo indicates he was alive when the mosaic was created). Almost opposite this church is Santo Stefano Rotondo, with a 7th-century mosaic commemorating two martyrs buried near by, and some gruesome frescos depicting torture.

Santa Maria ➕ Off map N11 ✉ Piazza della Navicella 12 ☎ 06 700 1519 ⏰ Daily 8.30–noon, 3.30–6 🚌 81, 673 to Via della Navicella 💶 Free

Santo Stefano ➕ Off map N11 ☎ 06 7049 3717 ⏰ Tue–Sat 9–1, 2–4.30, Mon 2–4.30, Oct–Mar; Mon–Sat 9–1, 3.30–6, May–Jun and Sep; Tue–Sat 9–12.30, Jul–Aug 🚌 81, 673 to Via della Navicella 💶 Free

SANTA PRASSEDE

The treasure of this church is its stunning, gold-encrusted mosaic commissioned by Pope Paschal I in 822 for his mother's mausoleum in the Cappella di San Zeno. So beautiful were the mosaics that in the Middle Ages the chapel became known as the Garden of Paradise. Similar Byzantine mosaics adorn the church's apse and triumphal arch.

✚ P9 ✉ Via Santa Prassede 9a ☎ 06 488 2456 🕓 Daily 7–noon, 4–6.30 🚌 16, 71, 75, 84 to Via Cavour–Piazza dell' Esquilino 💵 Free

SANTA PUDENZIANA

Built in the 4th century but much altered over the years, this church was reputedly raised over the house of the Roman senator Pudens, site of St. Peter's conversion of the senator's daughters, Pudenziana and Prassede. Its prized apse mosaic dates from this period, an early Christian depiction of a golden-robed Christ, the Apostles and two women presumed to be Prassede and Pudenziana.

✚ N8 ✉ Via Urbana 160 ☎ 06 481 4622 🕓 Mon–Sat 8–noon, 3–6, Sun 9–noon, 3–6 🚊 Termini 🚌 70, 71 to Via A de Pretis or 75, 84 to Via Cavour–Piazza dell' Esquilino 💵 Free

SANTI COSMA E DAMIANO

This church is part of the former Forum of Vespasian, one of the Imperial Fora, although a 1632 rebuilding wiped out all but a few vestiges of its original classical and medieval splendour. Chief among the surviving treasures is the 6th-century Byzantine mosaic in the apse, *The Second Coming*, a work whose mastery of colour and pattern influenced Roman and other mosaicists for centuries to come.

✚ L10 ✉ Via dei Fori Imperiali ☎ 06 699 1540 🕓 Daily 8–1, 4–7 (hours may vary) 🚌 All routes to Piazza Venezia and 60, 75, 85, 87, 117, 175, 810, 850 to Via Fori Imperiali 💵 Free

Mosaics in Cappella di San Zeno, Santa Prassede

SANT' AGNESE (ST. AGNES)

St. Agnes, who was martyred in Piazza Navona and buried near Sant' Agnese, was one of the most popular early Christian martyrs, despite the recorded fact that she failed to take a bath in the 13 years she was alive (such was her modesty). According to legend, this beautiful girl was martyred for refusing to marry the son of a pagan governor of the city. As an earlier punishment she was thrown into a brothel, but as she was about to be paraded naked her hair grew miraculously to spare her blushes. St. Agnes's steadfastness made her a symbol of Christian chastity, and her tomb became a place of pilgrimage particularly venerated by Roman women.

Mosaics in Santa Prassede

Churches

SANTA MARIA DELLA CONCEZIONE

Rome's most ghoulish sight lurks behind an unassuming façade in the unlikely surroundings of

Santa Maria in Cosmedin

the Via Vittorio Veneto. Lying in the crypt of Santa Maria della Concezione are the remains of 4,000 Capuchin monks, some still dressed in jaunty clothes, the bones of others crafted into macabre chandeliers and bizarre wall decorations. The bodies were originally buried in soil especially imported from Jerusalem. When this ran out they were left uncovered, a practice that continued until 1870. The church was built in 1624 by Cardinal Antonio Barberini, brother of Urban VIII, a Capuchin friar who lies buried before the main altar under a cheerful legend: '*hic jacet pulvis cinis et nihil*' ('here lie dust, ashes and nothing'). The church is known for Guido Reni's painting *St. Michael Trampling the Devil*, in which the Devil is reputedly a portrait of the Pamphilj Pope Innocent X.

➕ L6 ✉ Via Vittorio Veneto 27 ☎ 06 487 1185 🕐 Church daily 7–noon, 4–7. Crypt (Cimitero dei Cappuccini) daily 9–noon, 3–6 🚌 52, 53, 80, 95, 116, 119 and other services to Via Vittorio Veneto 🎫 Free (donation to visit crypt)

SANTA MARIA IN COSMEDIN

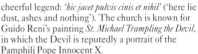

LA BOCCA DELLA VERITÀ

The 'Mouth of Truth' is a gaping marble mouth set in a stone face. Anyone suspected of lying–particularly a woman accused of adultery–would have his or her right hand forced into the maw. Legend claims that in the case of dissemblers the mouth would clamp shut and sever their fingers. To give credence to the story a priest supposedly hid behind the stone to hit the fingers of those known to be guilty.

This lovely old medieval church—one of the most atmospheric in the city—is best known for the Bocca della Verità, a weather-beaten stone face (of the sea god Oceanus) once used by the ancient Romans as a drain cover. Inside, the church has a beautiful floor, twin pulpits, a bishop's throne and a stone choir screen, all done in fine Cosmati stone inlay. Most date from the 12th century, a little earlier than the impressive *baldacchino* (altar canopy), which was built by Deodato di Cosma in 1294. Tucked away in a room off the right aisle is the mosaic *Adoration of the Magi*, almost all that remains of an 8th-century Greek church on the site.

➕ J11 ✉ Piazza Bocca della Verità ☎ 06 678 1419 🕐 Daily 9–7, Apr–Sep; 10–noon, 3–5, Oct–Mar 🚌 30, 44, 81, 95, 170 and other routes to Piazza Bocca della Verità or Lungotevere Pierleoni 🎫 Free

ROME
where to...

EAT

SHOP

BE ENTERTAINED

STAY

Expensive Restaurants

PRICES

Approximate price per person for a meal, including wine:

Expensive   over €50

Mid-Range   €30–50

Budget   under €30

All the eating establishments listed are located in, or close by, the *centro storico* ('historical centre') unless otherwise stated.

THE MENU

Starters are called antipasti; first course (soup, pasta or risotto) is *il primo*; and main meat and fish dishes are *il secondo*. Salads (*insalata*) and vegetables (*contorni*) are ordered (and often eaten) separately. Desserts are *dolci*, with cheese (*formaggio*) or fruit (*frutta*) to follow. If no menu card is offered, ask for *la lista* or *il menù*. A set-price menu (*un menù turistico*) may seem good value, but portions are usually small and the food is invariably poor—usually just spaghetti with a tomato sauce, followed by a piece of chicken and fruit.

AGATA E ROMEO

It is worth putting up with a less-than-perfect position south of Termini because this cosy, family-run restaurant serves some of the city's best and most imaginative modern Roman cooking.

➕ F6 ✉ Via Carlo Alberto ☎ 06 446 6115 ⏰ Mon–Fri 1–2.30, 8–11; closed 2 weeks in Jan and Aug 🚌 70, 71, 360 to Via Carlo Alberto

ALBERTO CIARLA

Located in the Trastevere district, this is among Rome's best fish restaurants, with a fine wine list. The food is elegantly presented, the candlelight lovely and the service impeccable.

➕ F11 ✉ Piazza San Cosimato 40 ☎ 06 581 8668 ⏰ Dinner only Mon–Sat. Closed 2 weeks in Aug and Jan 🚌 H, 8, 630, 780 to Viale di Trastevere

CHECCHINO DAL 1887

Robust appetites are required for the menu at this Testaccio establish-ment. Quintessential Roman dishes relying largely on offal are the speciality. Reservations advisable.

➕ Off map K11 ✉ Via Monte Testaccio 30 ☎ 06 574 6318 ⏰ Tue–Sat 12.30–3, 8–11; closed Aug 🚌 3, 60, 75, 118 to Piramide

IL CONVIVIO

The Troiani brothers from Italy's Marche region have created a tranquil little restaurant with a reputation for innovative and subtly flavoured modern dishes.

➕ G7 ✉ Vicolo dei Soldati 31 ☎ 06 686 9432 ⏰ Tue–Sat 1–2.30, 8–10.30, Mon 8–10.30 🚌 30, 70, 81, 87, 116, 492 to Corso del Rinascimento

LA ROSETTA

An exclusive fish and seafood restaurant whose popularity means reservations are a must.

➕ H7 ✉ Via della Rosetta 8–9 ☎ 06 686 1002 ⏰ Mon–Fri 1–3, 8–11.30, Sat 8–11.30; closed 2 weeks in Aug 🚌 119 to Piazza della Rotonda or 70, 81, 87, 90 to Corso del Rinascimento

SABATINI

Once Rome's most famous restaurant, Sabatini is still favoured for its reliable food and lovely setting, though prices are higher than the cooking deserves. Reservations are essential.

➕ G10 ✉ Piazza Santa Maria in Trastevere 13 (and Vicolo Santa Maria in Trastevere 18) ☎ 06 581 2026 or 06 581 8307) ⏰ Mon, Tue, Thu–Sun noon–2.30, 7.30–11; closed Aug 🚌 H, 8, 780 to Piazza Sidney Sonnino or 23, 280 to Lungotevere Sanzio

VECCHIA ROMA

In a pretty piazza and perfect for an alfresco meal on a summer evening. Although the 18th-century interior is also captivating, prices are rather high for what is only straightforward and reliable Roman cooking.

➕ J9 ✉ Piazza Campitelli 18 ☎ 06 686 4604 ⏰ Mon, Tue, Thu–Sun 1–3, 8–11; closed 3 weeks in Aug 🚌 All services to Via Arenula or Piazza Venezia

Mid-Range Restaurants

AL 34

Roman and southern Italian cooking, and a romantic, candelit intimacy. Close to Via Condotti and the Spanish Steps.
✚ J5 ✉ Via Mario de' Fiori 34 ☎ 06 679 5091 🕐 Tue–Sun 12.30–3, 7.30–11; closed 3 weeks in Aug 🚇 Spagna 🚌 119

CICCIA BOMBA

An excellent option amid the plethora of restaurants around Piazza Navona. Simple wooden tables, efficient service, and good Roman food at reasonable prices for this area.
✚ C5 ✉ Via dell Governo Vecchio 76 ☎ 06 6880 2108 🕐 Thu–Tue 12.30–3, 7.30–11.30; closed 2 weeks in Aug 🚌 All services to Corso del Rinascimento or Corso Vittorio Emanuele II

'GUSTO

A chic, modern restaurant on two levels where you can eat pizzas, salads and other light meals downstairs or fuller meals upstairs. There is also a good kitchenware shop.
✚ D5 ✉ Piazza Augusto Imperatore 9 ☎ 06 322 6273 🕐 Tue–Sun 1–3, 7.30–1 🚌 81 to Via Tomacelli or 117, 119 to Via del Corso

IL BACARO

Tiny but gracious restaurant north of the Pantheon; can be noisy, but the light, modern pan-Italian cooking is excellent.
✚ H7 ✉ Via degli Spagnoli 27, near Piazza delle Coppelle ☎ 06 686 4110 🕐 Mon–Sat 8am–11.30pm; closed Aug 🚇 Spagna 🚌 119

NERONE

A small, friendly, old-fashioned trattoria just a few steps north of the Colosseum that is best known for its antipasti buffet and simple Abruzzese cooking. Has a handful of outside tables.
✚ M10 ✉ Via delle Terme di Tito 96 ☎ 06 481 7952 🕐 Mon–Sat noon–3, 7–11; closed Aug 🚇 Colosseo 🚌 60, 75, 85, 87, 117, 175, 810, 850 to Piazza del Colosseo

PARIS

An extremely popular and elegant little restaurant just south of Piazza Santa Maria in Trastevere, and known for its fish, pastas and Roman cuisine. Outside tables for alfresco dining. Reserve ahead.
✚ G11 ✉ Piazza San Callisto 7a ☎ 06 581 5378 🕐 Tue–Sat 12.30–3, 8–11, Sun 12.30–3; closed 3 weeks in Aug 🚌 H, 8, 780 to Piazza Sidney Sonnino or 23, 280 to Lungotevere Sanzio

SORA LELLA

Founded by the legendary actress Sora Lella, and now presided over by her son and nephews, this is a two-room, wood-panelled former trattoria on the Isola Tiberina. Roman cooking, with menu and daily specials.
✚ H10 ✉ Via Ponte Quattro Capi 16 ☎ 06 686 1601 🕐 Mon–Sat 12.30–2.30, 7.30–10.30; closed Aug 🚌 23, 23, 63, 280 to Lungotevere dei Cenci or Lungotevere degli Anguillara

ROMAN SPECIALITIES

Roman favourites–though they are by no means confined to the city–include pastas like *bucatini all'Amatriciana* (tomato sauce, salt pork and chilli peppers); *spaghetti alla carbonara* (egg, bacon, pepper and cheese); and *gnocchi alla Romana* (small potato or semolina dumplings with tomato or butter). The best-known main course is *saltimbocca alla Romana* (veal scallops with ham and sage, cooked in wine and butter). Also traditional are *trippa* (tripe), *cervelli* (brains) and *coda alla vaccinara* (oxtail).

Budget Restaurants

RESTAURANT ETIQUETTE

Italians have a strongly developed sense of how to behave, which applies in restaurants as much as anywhere else. It is considered bad form to order only one course in any restaurant—if that is what you want, go to a pizzeria.

ANTICA BIRRERIA FRATELLI TEMPERA

Ideal for a simple lunch or dinner. Original art-nouveau interior and a large beer hall.
✚ K8 ✉ Via di San Marcello 19 ☎ 06 678 6203 🕐 Daily noon–midnight 🚌 44, 46, 64, 70, 81, 87 and all other buses to Piazza Venezia

AUGUSTO

One of Trastevere's last remaining inexpensive and authentic family-run trattorias, with 50 places. No credit cards.
✚ G10 ✉ Piazza de' Renzi 15 ☎ 06 580 3798 🕐 Mon–Sat 1–3.30, 8–11; closed Aug 🚌 23, 280 to Lungotevere Sanzio or H, 8, 780 to Piazza Sidney Sonnino

DA FRANCESCO

A simple restaurant near Piazza Navona, which over the years has never lost its appeal, thanks to a warm, friendly atmosphere, good food and low prices. No reservations so arrive early to be sure of a place.
✚ C5 ✉ Piazza del Fico ☎ 06 686 4009 🕐 Wed–Mon noon–3, 7–1 🚌 64 and other services to Chiesa Nuova on Corso Vittorio Emanuele II

DAL TOSCANO

Large trattoria with Tuscan food in Vatican City. Particularly known for its meats (including classic *bistecca alla fiorentina*) and its wood-fired grill.
✚ D5 ✉ Via Germanico 58 ☎ 06 3972 5717 🕐 Tue–Sun 12.30–2.30, 7.30–11; closed parts of Jan and Aug 🚇 Ottaviano 🚌 23, 49, 81 to Piazza del Risorgimento

FIASCHETTERIE BELTRAMME DA CESARETTO

In a historical monument, with a fine courtyard outside. Inside, shared tables keep things convivial. Close to the Spanish Steps.
✚ J5 ✉ Via della Croce 39 ☎ No phone 🕐 Mon–Sat 12.15–3, 7.30–11; closed 2 weeks in Aug 🚇 Spagna 🚌 119 to Piazza di Spagna or 81, 90 to Via del Corso

FILETTI DI BACCALÀ

At this tiny place with Formica tables you wash down cod with plenty of beer or crisp local wine.
✚ G9 ✉ Largo dei Librari 88, off Via dei Giubbonari ☎ 06 686 4018 🕐 Mon–Sat 5.30–11; closed Aug and 1 week Dec–Jan 🚌 H, 8, 63, 630, 780 to Via Arenula

GRAPPOLO D'ORO

An unspoiled trattoria favoured by locals and foreign residents for decades. The menu has *pasta all'amatriciana* and *scaloppine* any way you like.
✚ G8 ✉ Piazza della Cancelleria 80 ☎ 06 689 7080 🕐 Tue–Sun 12.30–2.30, 7.30–10.30, Mon 12.30–2.30; closed Aug 🚌 46, 62, 64 to Corso Vittorio Emanuele II

PIZZA CIRO

The pizzas and pasta here are far better than the lurid murals on the walls. A good bet in busy and generally expensive streets close to Via Condotti.
✚ D5 ✉ Via della Mercede 43 ☎ 06 678 6015 🕐 Daily 11.30am–1.30am 🚇 Spagna 🚌 All services to Via del Corso and Via del Tridente

Pizzerias

BAFFETTO (€)

Rome's most famous pizzeria. A tiny, hole-in-the-wall classic that has retained its atmosphere and low prices despite its fame. Expect to wait for a table.

🔲 G8 ⊠ Via del Governo Vecchio 114, corner of Via Sora ☎ 06 686 1617 🕐 Daily 6.30 –1am; closed Aug 🚌 46, 62, 64 to Corso Vittorio Emanuele II

CORALLO (€)

This stylish pizzeria is convenient to Piazza Navona. Full meals also available.

🔲 G7 ⊠ Via del Corallo 10, off Via del Governo Vecchio ☎ 06 6830 7703 🕐 Tue–Sun 7.30pm–1.30am; closed 1 week in Aug 🚌 46, 62, 64 to Corso Vittorio Emanuele II

DA VITTORIO (€)

Tiny Neapolitan-run Trastevere pizzeria that makes a good standby if Ivo (see below) is busy.

🔲 F11 ⊠ Via di San Cosimato 14a, off Piazza San Calisto ☎ 06 580 0353 🕐 Mon–Sat 7pm–midnight 🚌 H, 8, 780 to Viale di Trastevere

EST! EST! EST! (€)

Among Rome's oldest pizzerias; worth the slight walk if you are staying near Stazione Termini.

🔲 M7 ⊠ Via Genova 32 ☎ 06 488 1107 🕐 Tue–Sun 6.30–11.30pm; closed Aug 🚇 Repubblica 🚌 H, 40, 60, 64, 70, 117, 170 to Via Nazionale

IVO (€)

The best-known of Trastevere's pizzerias. Lines are common but turnover is quick.

🔲 G11 ⊠ Via di San Francesco a Ripa 158 ☎ 06 581 7082 🕐 Wed–Mon 5.30–2am; closed 3 weeks in Aug 🚌 H, 8, 780 to Viale di Trastevere

LA CAPRICCIOSA (€)

Roomy and rather stylish, with a terrace for alfresco eating. Reputedly the birthplace of the *capricciosa* pizza (ham, egg, artichoke and olives). Full meals also served; pizzas are available evenings only.

🔲 J5 ⊠ Largo dei Lombardi 8, Via del Corso ☎ 06 687 8480 🕐 Mon, Wed–Sun 12.15am–3pm, 7pm–12.30am; closed 3 weeks in Aug 🚇 Spagna 🚌 81, 119 to Via del Corso-Via della Croce

LEONCINO (€)

Little has changed in the wonderful old-fashioned interior for over 30 years. The retro feel has made it very popular, so expect to wait in line.

🔲 J6 ⊠ Via del Leoncino 28, Piazza San Lorenzo in Lucina ☎ 06 687 6306 🕐 Mon–Tue, Thu–Fri 1–2.30pm, 7pm–midnight, Sat 7pm–midnight 🚇 Spagna 🚌 81, 119 to Via del Corso-Via Tomacelli

PANATTONI (€)

Big, bright and often busy, Panattoni is known locally as 'L'Obitorio' (The Morgue) on account of its cold marble tables. Seating also outside on Viale di Trastevere.

🔲 G11 ⊠ Viale di Trastevere 53 ☎ 06 580 0919 🕐 Thu–Tue 6.30pm–2am; closed 3 weeks in Aug 🚌 H, 8, 780 to Viale di Trastevere

---

PRICES

Where appropriate, an indication of the cost of an establishment is given by € signs:

€€€ = up to €50

€€ = €30–50

€ = under €3

THE BILL

The bill (check), *il conto*, usually includes extras such as *servizio* (service). Iniquitous cover charges (*pane e coperto*) have now been outlawed, but some restaurants still try to get round the regulations. Only pay for bread (*pane*) if you have asked for it. Proper receipts–not a scrawled piece of paper–must be given by law. If you receive a scrap of paper, which is more likely in a pizzeria, and have doubts about the total, be sure to ask for a proper receipt (*una fattura* or *una ricevuta*).

World Cuisines

AFRICA (€)

A long-established restaurant close to Termini, catering mainly to Rome's Ethiopian and Eritrean population with dishes such as *injera* (pancakes served with meat).
➕ P6 ✉ Via Gaeta 26 ☎ 06 494 1077 🕐 Tue–Sun noon–3.30, 7.30–11; closed 2 weeks in Aug 🚌 16, 38, 217, 360 to Via Volturno and all buses to Termini

BIRRERIA VIENNESE (€)

An authentic beer house east of the centre with a wide range of Austro-German specialities.
➕ J5 ✉ Via della Croce 21 ☎ 06 679 5569 🕐 Daily 12.30–midnight 🚇 Spagna 🚌 81, 90 to Via del Corso or 119 to Piazza di Spagna

CHARLY'S SAUCIÈRE (€€)

Cosy and established, offering reliable French and Swiss staples.
➕ P11 ✉ Via di San Giovanni in Laterano 268–270 ☎ 06 7049 5666 🕐 Tue–Sat 7.45–11; closed 2 weeks in Aug 🚌 85, 117, 850 to Via San Giovanni in Laterano

GIGGETTO (€)

A famous Romano-Jewish restaurant in the Ghetto district; almost as good and cheaper than Piperno.
➕ J10 ✉ Via Portico d'Ottavia 21a ☎ 06 686 1105 🕐 Tue–Sun 12.30–2.30, 7.30–10.30 🚌 8 to Via Arenula and 46, 62, 63, 70 and other services to Largo di Torre Argentina

HASEKURA (€–€€)

Rome's best Japanese food; good set-price menus, with the Forum and Colosseum close by.
➕ E6 ✉ Via dei Serpenti 27 ☎ 06 483 648 🕐 Mon–Sat noon–2.30, 7–10.30; closed Aug 🚇 Cavour 🚌 71, 84 to Via Cavour

L'EAU VIVE (€€)

A bizarre dining experience. The predominantly French food is served by nuns (► panel). Politicians, celebrities and locals come to enjoy the food and the beautiful 16th-century frescoed dining rooms.
➕ H8 ✉ Via Monterone 85 ☎ 06 654 1095 or 06 6880 1095 🕐 Mon–Sat 12.30–3.30, 7.30–10; closed Aug 🚌 8, 46, 62, 63, 64, 70, 81, 87, 186, 492 to Largo di Torre Argentina

MAGNA ROMA (€€€)

This intriguing restaurant attempts to recreate the dishes, wines and atmosphere of ancient Rome. There is even a resident archaeologist on hand to answer questions.
➕ E7 ✉ Via Capo d'Africa 26 ☎ 06 700 9800 🕐 Daily 6–11.30 (also noon–2.30 Apr–Sep) 🚇 Colesseo 🚌 All services to Piazza del Colosseo

PIPERNO (€€)

Much Roman cuisine is based on the city's Jewish culinary traditions. The famous and resolutely traditional Piperno has been a temple to Romano-Jewish cuisine for over a century. Reserve ahead.
➕ H10 ✉ Via Monte de' Cenci 9 ☎ 06 6880 6629/2772 🕐 Tue–Sat 12.15–2.30, 8–10.30, Sun 12.15–3; closed Aug 🚌 8 to Via Arenula and 8, 46, 62, 63, 64, 70, 81, 87, 492 to Largo di Torre Argentina

Gelaterie

ALBERTO PICA

Only around 20 flavours, but of excellent quality; try the house specialities like green apple (*mele verde*) and Sicilian citrus (*agrumi di Sicilia*).

🚩 H9 ✉ Via della Seggiola 12, Cenci ☎ 06 686 8405 🕐 Mon–Sat 8am–1.30am (also Sun 4pm–2am, Apr–Oct); closed 2 weeks in Aug 🚌 8 to Via Arenula and 8, 46, 62, 63, 64, 70, 81, 87, 186, 492 to Largo di Torre Argentina

DA MIRELLA

Sells *granita*: crushed ice drenched in juice or syrup. The flavourings in this kiosk have been refined over many years; the ice is still hand-ground.

🚩 H10 ✉ Lungotevere Anguillara, Ponte Cestio 🕐 Daily 8am–late, May–Sep 🚌 23, 280

GELATERIA DELLA PALMA

A big, brash place behind the Pantheon. Cakes and chocolates, plus over 100 flavours of ice cream—many of them a little wild.

🚩 H7 ✉ Via della Maddalena 20 ☎ 06 6880 6752 🕐 Daily 9am–midnight 🚌 119 to Piazza della Rotonda

GIOLITTI

For years Giolitti was the king of Roman ice cream. Standards have slipped slightly, but the ice cream, coffee and cakes are still excellent value.

🚩 H7 ✉ Via Uffici del Vicario 40 ☎ 06 699 1243 🕐 Tue–Fri, Sun 7am–12.30am, Sat 7am–2am 🚌 119 to Piazza della Rotonda or 62, 80, 81, 85, 95, 117, 119, 160, 175 and other services to Via del Corso

IL GELATO DI SAN CRISPINO

The best ice cream in Rome. The fresh ingredients mean flavours vary according to season.

🚩 K7 ✉ Via della Panetteria 42 ☎ 06 679 3924 🕐 Daily noon–12.30/1.30am 🚌 52, 53, 56, 58 and other routes to Via del Corso and Via del Tritone

PALAZZO DEL FREDDO

A Roman institution with historic interior and superb ice cream; try *caterinetta*, the honey and vanilla house speciality.

🚩 F6 ✉ Via Principe Eugenio 65–7 ☎ 06 446 4740 🕐 Tue–Sat noon–midnight 🚇 Vittorio 🚌 5, 14 to Via Principe Eugenio

SACCHETTI

Family-run bar in Trastevere also good for cakes and pastries.

🚩 F11 ✉ Piazza San Cosimato 61–2 ☎ 06 581 5374 🕐 Tue–Sun 5am–11pm 🚌 H, 8, 780 to Viale di Trastevere

SAN FILIPPO

A quiet bar in Parioli among the best *gelaterie* in the city. Zabaglione is emperor of the 60-odd flavours.

🚩 Off map N1 ✉ Via di Villa San Filippo 8–10 ☎ 06 807 9314 🕐 Tue–Sun 7.30am–10pm/midnight 🚌 Bus or tram 30 to Piazza Ungheria

TRE SCALINI

Known for its chocolate-studded *tartufo* (the best chocolate-chip ice cream).

🚩 G7 ✉ Piazza Navona 28–32 ☎ 06 6880 1996 🕐 Thu–Tue 8am–1am 🚌 30, 70, 81, 87, 116 and other services to Corso del Rinascimento

BUYING ICE CREAM

Ice cream (*gelato*) in a proper *gelateria* is sold either in a cone (*un cono*) or a paper cup (*una coppa*). Specify which you want and then decide how much you wish to pay: sizes of cone and cup go up in price bands, usually starting small and ending enormous. You can choose up to two or three flavours (more in bigger tubs) and will usually be asked if you want a swirl of cream (*panna*) to round things off.

Bars by Day

BAR ETIQUETTE

You almost always pay a premium to sit down (inside or outside) and to enjoy the privilege of waiter service in Roman bars. If you stand—which is less expensive–the procedure is to pay for what you want first at the cash desk (*la cassa*). You then take your receipt (*lo scontrino*) to the bar and repeat your order (a tip slapped down on the bar will work wonders in attracting the bar person's attention). Pastry shops, cafés and ice cream parlours often double as excellent all-around bars to be enjoyed during the day. They include Giolitti and Tre Scalini (► 69), Camilloni and Sant' Eustachio (► 71).

AUTOGRILL

A big century-old bar with a huge and varied clientele. Self-service selection of hot and cold food.
➕ J6 ✉ Via del Corso 181 ☎ 06 678 9135 🕐 Daily 7.30am–11pm 🚇 Spagna 🚌 119 to Piazza Augusto Imperatore

BAR DELLA PACE

Extremely trendy, but quieter by day, when you can sit outside or enjoy the 19th-century mirror-and-mahogany interior.
➕ G7 ✉ Via della Pace 3, off Piazza Navona ☎ 06 686 1216 🕐 Daily 9am–2am; closed Mon am 🚌 30, 70, 81, 87, 116 to Corso del Rinascimento

BAR FRATTINA

A perfect retreat from shopping near Piazza di Spagna. Coffee, snacks, light meals and decadent puddings in a bustling atmosphere; outside tables.
➕ K6 ✉ Via Frattina 142 🕐 Mon–Sat 8am–9pm 🚇 Spagna 🚌 119 to Piazza di Spagna

CANOVA

Canova is pricier and less atmospheric than nearby Rosati, though its sunny outside tables on Piazza del Popolo provide a welcome pause.
➕ H4 ✉ Piazza del Popolo 16 ☎ 06 361 2231 🕐 Daily 7.30am–12.30am 🚇 Flaminio or Spagna 🚌 119 to Piazza del Popolo

CIAMPINI

You can sit here for hours facing Bernini's Fontana dei Quattro Fiumi (► 56), but watch your bill.
➕ G7 ✉ Piazza Navona 94–100 ☎ 06 686 1547 🕐 Tue–Sun 8.30am–12.30am 🚌 46, 62, 64 to Corso Vittorio Emanuele II or 30, 70, 81, 87, 116 to Corso del Rinascimento

DONEY

Most bars famous in the *dolce vita* 1950s are now tacky and expensive, but this one is as tasteful and inviting as ever.
➕ M5 ✉ Via Vittorio Veneto 145 ☎ 06 4708 2805 🕐 Tue–Sat 8am–1am 🚇 Barberini 🚌 52, 53, 63, 80, 95 to Via Vittorio Veneto

LATTERIA DEL GALLO

Marble tables and 1940s decor. Try the big, sticky cakes and steaming hot chocolate.
➕ G9 ✉ Vicolo del Gallo 4 ☎ 06 686 5091 🕐 Thu–Tue 8.30–2, 5–midnight 🚌 46, 62, 64 to Corso Vittorio Emanuele II

ROSATI

In a superb location with wonderful coffee, cocktails, cakes and pastries (from vintage ovens) and a glittering 1922 art-nouveau interior.
➕ H4 ✉ Piazza del Popolo 5 ☎ 06 322 5859 🕐 Daily 7.30am–midnight 🚇 Flaminio or Spagna 🚌 119 to Piazza del Popolo

TRASTÈ

This chic tea and coffee shop in Trastevere also serves light meals. People come to chat, read the papers and pass the time.
➕ G10 ✉ Via della Lungaretta 76 ☎ 06 589 4430 🕐 Tue–Sun 5pm–12.30am 🚌 H, 8, 780 to Piazza Sidney Sonnino

Coffee & Pastries

ANTICO CAFFÈ BRASILE

Superb variety of beans and ground coffee sold from huge sacks or at the bar. Try the 'Pope's blend': John Paul II bought his coffee here before his pontificate.
➕ M9 ✉ Via dei Serpenti 23 ☎ 06 488 2319 🕑 Mon–Sat 6.30am–8.30pm 🚇 60, 63, 64, 70, 117, 170 to Via Nazionale or 75, 84, 117 to Via Cavour

BABINGTON'S TEA ROOMS

Only tourists and the well-heeled visit Babington's, established by a pair of English spinsters in 1896. Prices are sky-high, but the tea (although not the cakes) is the best in Rome.
➕ K5 ✉ Piazza di Spagna 23 ☎ 06 678 6027 🕑 Wed–Mon 9am–8pm 🚇 Spagna 🚌 119 to Piazza di Spagna

CAFÉ NOTEGEN

This friendly old family-run café has a loyal local clientele. Excellent light lunches and all-day snacks to take away or eat in.
➕ J5 ✉ Via del Babuino 159 ☎ 06 320 0855 🕑 Mon–Sat 7am–midnight, Sun 10.30am–midnight 🚇 Spagna 🚌 119 to Piazza del Popolo

CAFFÈ FARNESE

Quieter and more elegant than the bars on the nearby Campo de' Fiori. Serves cakes, ice creams and light snacks as well as drinks. Also has tables on the cobbled street outside.
➕ G9 ✉ Via dei Baullari 106–7, at Piazza Farnese ☎ 06 6880 2125 🕑 Daily 7am–2am 🚌 8, 46, 62, 64

CAFFÈ GRECO

Rome's most famous café, founded in 1767. Plush, but no longer the best.
➕ J5 ✉ Via Condotti 86 ☎ 06 679 1700 🕑 Daily 8am–8.30pm 🚇 Spagna 🚌 119 to Piazza di Spagna or 52, 53, 61, 71, 85, 160 to Piazza San Silvestro

CAMILLONI

A long-time rival to Sant' Eustachio, with which it shares a piazza.
➕ H8 ✉ Piazza Sant' Eustachio 54 ☎ 06 271 6068 🕑 Tue–Sun 8am–9pm 🚌 119 to Piazza della Rotonda or 30, 70, 81, 87, 116 to Corso del Rinascimento

DAGNINO

Not even the customers have changed in this superb 1950s *pasticceria*. Fine Sicilian specialities, lemon ices and ice cream.
➕ N6 ✉ Galleria Esedra, Via Vittorio Emanuele Orlando 75 ☎ 06 481 8660 🕑 Daily 7am–10pm 🚇 Spagna 🚌 H, 40, 60, 64, 70, 71, 84, 86, 90, 170 to Piazza della Repubblica

LA TAZZA D'ORO

The 'Cup of Gold' sells only coffee, and probably the city's best espresso.
➕ H7 ✉ Via degli Orfani 84 ☎ 06 678 9792 🕑 Mon–Sat 7am–8pm 🚌 119 to Piazza della Rotonda or 30, 70, 81, 87, 116, 186 to Corso del Rinascimento

SANT' EUSTACHIO

Excellent coffee served in a pleasant interior and tables outside.
➕ H8 ✉ Piazza Sant' Eustachio 82 ☎ 06 6880 2048 🕑 Daily 8.30am–1am 🚌 119 to Piazza della Rotonda or 30, 70, 81, 87, 116 to Corso del Rinascimento

BREAKFAST AND COFFEE

Breakfast in Rome consists of a sweet, sometimes cream-filled croissant (*un cornetto* or *brioche*) washed down with a cappuccino or the longer and milkier *caffè latte*. At other times espresso, a short kick-start of caffeine, is the coffee of choice (Italians never drink cappuccino after lunch or dinner). Decaffeinated coffee is *caffè Hag*, iced coffee *caffè freddo* and American-style coffee (long and watery) *caffè Americano*. Other varieties include *caffè corretto* (with a dash of grappa or brandy) and *caffè macchiato* (espresso 'stained' with a dash of milk).

Footwear

SHOPPING AREAS

Although Rome's individual neighbourhoods have their own butchers, bakers and corner shops (*alimentari*), most of the city's quality and speciality shops are concentrated in specific areas. Via Condotti and its surrounding grid of streets (Via Frattina, Via Borgognana and Via Bocca di Leone) contain most of the big names in men's and women's fashion, accessories, jewellery and luxury goods. In nearby Via del Babuino and Via Margutta, the emphasis is on top antiques, paintings, sculpture and modern glassware and lighting. Via della Croce, which runs south from Piazza di Spagna, is known for its food shops, while Via del Corso, which bisects the northern half of central Rome, is home to bargain mid-range clothes, shoes and accessories shops. For inexpensive shops visit Via del Tritone and Via Nazionale. Nice areas to browse for antiques, even if you are not buying, include Via Giulia, Via dei Coronari, Via dell'Orso, Via dei Soldati and Via del Governo Vecchio.

BATA

A well-known and respected chain devoted predominantly to casual footwear. It also sells children's shoes.
✉ Via dei Due Macelli 45
☎ 06 679 1570 🕐 Mon–Sat 9.30–7.30, Sun 3.30–7.30;
✉ Via Nazionale 89
☎ 06 482 4529 🕐 Mon–Sat 9.30–7.30, Sun 3.30–7.30

BORINI

This family-run business creates restrained and elegant handmade shoes in classic and contemporary styles at surprisingly reasonable prices. The quality is excellent, too.
✉ Via dei Due Macelli 45
☎ 06 687 5670 🕐 Tue–Sat 9–7.30, Mon 3.30–7.30; closed 2 weeks in Aug

BRUNO MAGLI

A middle to upmarket quality chain with a choice of formal and some casual styles.
✉ Via del Gambero 1
☎ 06 679 3802
🕐 Daily 9.30–7.30;
✉ Aeroporto di Fiumicino
☎ 06 6501 1730
🕐 Daily 9.30–7.30

CAMPANILE

This shop, in chic Via Condotti, is dedicated to the most elegant (and expensive) styles. Men's and women's shoes, plus a range of leather bags.
✉ Via Condotti 58 ☎ 06 678 3041 🕐 Tue–Sat 9.30–7.30, Mon 3.30–7.30

FAUSTO SANTINI

An iconoclast who designs witty, innovative and occasionally bizarre shoes for the young and daring.
✉ Via Frattina 120–1
☎ 06 678 4114 🕐 Mon–Sat 10–7.30

FERRAGAMO

An established family firm; probably Italy's most renowned shoe shop, with branches on exclusive shopping streets the world over.
✉ Via Condotti 73–4
☎ 06 679 1565;
✉ Via Condotti 65 ☎ 06 678 1130 🕐 Tue–Sat 10–7, Mon 3–7.30

FRATELLI ROSSETTI

This family company, founded 30 years ago by the brothers Renzo and Renato, rivals Ferragamo as Italy's best shoe shop, and is slightly cheaper. Classic and current styles for men and women.
✉ Via Borgognona 5a
☎ 06 678 2676 🕐 Tue–Sat 9.30–7.30, Mon 3.30–7.30

POLLINI

Up-to-the-minute boots and bags in lively styles for men and women.
✉ Via Frattina 22–4
☎ 06 678 9028 🕐 Tue–Sat 10–1, 3–7.30, Mon 3–7.30

TOD'S

Distinctive and much-coveted driving shoes made Tod's a big fashion label. A showcase shop for an ever-expanding range of quality shoes, both smart and informal as well as a small range of other well-made leather goods.
✉ Via Borgognona 45
☎ 06 678 6828 🕐 Daily 10–7.30

Accessories & Leather Goods

BORSALINO

This shop should be your first port of call if you are looking to buy a hat.
✉ Piazza del Popolo 20
☎ 06 323 3353
🕐 Mon–Sat 9–8

CALZA E CALZE

A cornucopia of socks, stockings and tights in every colour and style imaginable.
✉ Via della Croce 78
🕐 Tue–Sat 9.30–1, 3.30–7.30, Mon 3.30–7.30

FENDI

A famous family-run high-fashion name whose burgeoning Via Borgognona shop deals in both clothes and fine leather goods.
✉ Via Borgognona 36–40
☎ 06 679 7641 🕐 Mon–Sat 10–7.30

FOGAL

A small shop crammed with a dazzling selection of stockings, socks and lingerie: choose between conservative or more innovative styles and colours.
✉ Via Condotti 55
☎ 06 678 4566 🕐 Tue–Sat 10–7.30, Mon 1–7

GUCCI

Recovering from the turmoil of the 1980s, when tax problems and feuds threatened to destroy the family business, this famous name is once more in the ascendant. Expensive and high-quality bags, shoes and leather goods are a feature of this elegant shop.

✉ Via Condotti 8 ☎ 06 679 0405 🕐 Tue–Sat 10–2, 3–7, Mon 3–7

LA PERLA

Italian lingerie is among the best in the world, and this reputation is more than upheld by La Perla. The wonderful fabrics and the variety of colours and styles, come in sizes to suit all.
✉ Via Condotti 79
☎ 06 6994 1934 🕐 Tue–Sat 9.30–7.30, Mon 3.30–7.30

MEROLA

Specialises in a wide range of highly priced gloves, scarves and stockings.
✉ Via del Corso 143
☎ 06 679 1961 🕐 Tue–Sat 9.30–7.30, Mon 3–7

SERGIO DI CORI

Romans who need gloves look no further than this tiny shop, which sells almost nothing else.
✉ Piazza di Spagna 53
☎ 06 678 4439 🕐 Mon–Sat 9.30–7.30

SERMONETA

Glove specialist: styles are innovative and colours bright—fuchsias, purples and vivid reds—although the shop is not as famous as nearby rival, Sergio di Cori.
✉ Piazza di Spagna 61
☎ 06 679 1960 🕐 Mon–Sat 9.30–7.30

SIRNI

Exquisite artisan-made bags and briefcases crafted on the premises.
✉ Via della Stelletta 33
☎ 06 6880 5248 🕐 Tue–Sat 9.30–1.30, 2–8, Mon 11–8

JEWELLERY

Jewellery, and lots of it, is a key part of any Roman woman's wardrobe. Gold, in particular, is popular, and is still worked in small artisans' studios in the Jewish Ghetto, around Via Giulia and Campo de' Fiori and on Via dei Coronari, Via dell'Orso and Via del Pellegrino. For the purchase of a lifetime, visit the most famous of Italian jewellers, Bulgari, whose shop at Via Condotti 10 is one of the most splendid in the city. For striking costume jewellery try Delettré (✉ Via Fontanella Borghese) or Bozart (✉ Via Bocca di Leone 4). For a more sober look visit Massoni (✉ Largo Carlo Goldoni 48), founded in 1790, or Petocchi (✉ Piazza di Spagna), jewellers to Italy's former royal family from 1861 to 1946.

Women's Fashion

SALES AND BARGAINING

Sales (*saldi*) in Rome are not always the bargains they can be in other major cities. That said, many shoe shops and top designers cut their prices drastically during summer and winter sales (mid-July to mid-September and January to mid-March). Other lures to get you into a shop, notably the offer of *sconti* (discounts) and *vendite promozionali* (promotional offers), rarely save you any money. While bargaining has all but died out, it can still occasionally be worth asking for a discount (*uno sconto*), particularly if you are paying cash (as opposed to using a credit card) for an expensive item, or if you are buying several items from one shop.

FENDI

From recent beginnings, the Fendi sisters have built a powerful fashion, perfume and accessories empire. Clothes are classic, sleek and stylish.
✉ Via Borgognona 36–40
☎ 06 679 7641 ⏰ Mon–Sat 10–7.30

GIANFRANCO FERRÈ

One of Italy's top designers. His Rome shop is known for its outlandish steel and black mosaic decor.
✉ Via Borgognona 6
☎ 06 679 7445 ⏰ Tue–Sat 9.30–7.30, Mon 3.30–7.30

GIANNI VERSACE

Flashier and trashier than Ferrè or Armani, Versace's bright, bold styles require panache.
✉ Via Borgognona 25 ☎ 06 696 661 ⏰ Tue–Sat 10–7.30, Mon 3.30–7.30

GIORGIO ARMANI

King of cut and classic, understated elegance. The slightly less expensive line is at Emporio Armani (➤ 75).
✉ Via Condotti 77
☎ 06 699 1460 ⏰ Mon 3.30–7.30, Tue–Sat 10–7

MARELLA

The showcase shop for the Marella label offers classic, well-made designs at reasonable prices that will appeal to young and old.
✉ Via Frattina 129–31
☎ 06 6992 3800 ⏰ Tue–Sat 10–7.30, Mon 3.30–7.30

LAURA BIAGIOTTI

Easy to wear, easy on the eye and less aggressively 'high fashion' than the other outlets in Via Borgognona.
✉ Via Borgognona 43–44
☎ 06 679 1205 ⏰ Tue–Sat 10–7.30, Mon 3.30–7.30

MAX MARA

A popular mid-range label known for reliable suits, separates, knitwear and bags and other accessories at fair prices. See also sister shop, Max & Co., at Via Condotti 46–46a.
✉ Via Condotti 17–19a
☎ 06 6992 2104 ⏰ Tue–Sat 10–7.30, Mon 3.30–7.30;
✉ Via Frattina 28 ☎ 06 679 3638 ⏰ Tue–Sat 10–7.30, Mon 3.30–7.30

TRUSSARDI

Flagship shop for another top name in Italian fashion with clothes in fine fabrics and a range of accessories.
✉ Via Condotti 49–50
☎ 06 678 2080 ⏰ Tue–Sat 10–7.30, Mon 3.30–7.30

VALENTINO

The maestro of Roman fashion has been dressing celebrities and the rich since 1959. For more affordable ready-to-wear creations visit Via Condotti and Via Bocca di Leone.
✉ Piazza Mignanelli 22
☎ 06 67 391 ⏰ Mon–Sat 10–7;
✉ Via Bocca di Leone 15
☎ 06 679 5862 ⏰ Mon–Sat 10–7;
✉ Via Condotti 13
☎ 06 6789 5862 ⏰ Mon–Sat 10–7;
✉ Via del Babuino 61 (Valentino Donna) ☎ 06 3600 1906
⏰ Mon–Sat 10–7

Men's Tailors & Clothes

BATTISTONI
This traditional tailor's shop has sold made-to-measure and ready-to-wear suits and shirts for over half a century. It also stocks well-made informal wear.
✉ Via Condotti 61a ☎ 06 697 6111 ⏰ Tue–Sat 10–7.30

DAVIDE CENCI
The country gentleman look—tweeds, brogues and muted classics—is hugely popular among Italian men. This enormous shop, established in 1926, caters to the trend with Burberry, Aquascutum and its own lines.
✉ Via Campo Marzio 1–7 ☎ 06 699 0681 ⏰ Tue–Sat 9–1, 3.30–7.30 (also Sat 10–7.30, Mon 3.30–7.30, May–Sep)

DIESEL
A large, modern mid-range shop aimed at the young or young at heart, which sells its fashionable own-label jeans, shirts and other informal wear.
✉ Via del Corso 186 ☎ 06 678 3933 ⏰ Tue–Sat 10.30–7.30, Sun 3–7.30, Mon 2–7.30 (hours can vary)

EMPORIO ARMANI
Relatively speaking, the cheaper way to buy Armani.
✉ Via del Babuino 139–40 ☎ 06 3660 2197 ⏰ Mon–Sat 10–7

ENZO CECI
Ready-to-wear high fashion.
✉ Via della Vite 52 ☎ 06 679 8882 ⏰ Tue–Sat 10–1.30, 3.30–7.30, Mon 3.30–7.30

ERMENEGILDO ZEGNA
Informal suits and jackets in exquisite, expensive fabrics. Also stocks shirts, sweaters and accessories.
✉ Via Borgognona 7e ☎ 06 678 9143 ⏰ Mon–Sat 10–7.30

PRADA
The flagship Rome store for the prestigious Milan-based label. Men's and women's clothes, shoes and accessories.
✉ Via Condotti 92–5 ☎ 06 679 0897 ⏰ Tue–Sat 10–7.30, Mon 3.30–7.30

SCHOSTAL
Conservative clothes and accessories, beautifully made in the finest fabrics. Surprisingly favourable prices, with courteous old-fashioned service.
✉ Via del Corso 158 ☎ 06 679 1240 ⏰ Tue–Sat 9.30–7.30, Mon 3.30–7.30

TESTA
Exquisite suits cut to appeal to a younger set, plus an excellent range of (mostly blue) shirts.
✉ Via Borgognona 13 ☎ 06 679 6174 ⏰ Tue–Sat 9.30–1.30, 3.30–7.30, Mon 3.30–7.30;
✉ Via Frattina 42 ☎ 06 679 0660 ⏰ Tue–Sat 9.30–1.30, 3.30–7.30, Mon 3.30–7.30

VALENTINO UOMO
Sober and conservative clothes in the finest materials from Rome's leading tailor.
✉ Via Condotti 12 ☎ 06 679 5862 ⏰ Mon–Sat 10–7;
✉ Via Bocca di Leone 15 ☎ 06 679 5862 ⏰ Mon–Sat 10–7

TOP PEOPLE'S TAILOR

While the young turn to the mainstream Milanese designers like Armani, Rome's older and more traditional élite still choose Battistoni for their sartorial needs. Giorgio Battistoni started out almost half a century ago as a shirtmaker but quickly graduated to the role of top-class tailor, dressing the city's older aristocracy and the more conservative hedonists of the late 1950s *dolce vita*. Clothes with the Battistoni label are still as prestigious as they were in the past and just as costly–a custom-made shirt starts at around €155.

Books & Stationery

FOREIGN NEWSPAPERS

Foreign newspapers can be bought at many newsstands (*edicole*) around the city. European editions of the *International Herald Tribune* and the *Financial Times* (and occasionally *USA Today*) hit the newsstands first thing in the morning with the Italian papers. Other foreign editions arrive at around 2.30pm on the day of issue, except for Sunday editions, which are not usually available until Monday morning. The best-stocked newsstands, which also include a wide range of foreign magazines and periodicals, are found in Piazza Colonna on Via del Corso, at Termini train station, and at the southern end of the Via Vittorio Veneto.

ECONOMY BOOK AND VIDEO CENTRE

American-run, Italy's largest English-language bookshop is an established fixture of expat life. New and second-hand titles. Fairly pricey.
✉ Via Torino 136 ☎ 06 474 6877 🕐 Mon–Sat 9–8; closed 1 week in Aug

FELTRINELLI

An Italy-wide bookshop chain with well-designed shelves displaying a broad range of Italian titles, and usually a reasonable choice of French-, German- and English-language books.
✉ Largo di Torre Argentina 5a ☎ 06 6880 3248 🕐 Mon–Sat 9–8, Sun 10–1.30, 4–7.30; ✉ Via del Babuino 39–41 ☎ 06 3600 1873 🕐 Mon–Sat 9–8, Sun 10–1.30, 4–7.30; ✉ Via Vittorio Emanuele II Orlando 78–81/84 ☎ 06 484 430 or 06 487 0171 🕐 Mon–Sat 9–8, Sun 10–1.30, 4–7.30

IL SIGILLO

Close to the Pantheon, this little shop specialises in fine pens, hand-printed stationery and a wide variety of objects covered in marbled paper.
✉ Via della Guglia 69 ☎ 06 678 9667 🕐 Daily 11–8

PINEIDER

Rome's most expensive and exclusive stationers. Virtually any design can be printed onto persona-lised visiting cards.
✉ Via dei Due Macelli 68 ☎ 06 678 9013 🕐 Tue–Sat 10–7.30, Mon 3–7.30; ✉ Via della Fontanella Borghese 22 ☎ 06 687 8369 🕐 Tue–Sat 10–7.30, Mon 3–7.30

POGGI

Vivid pigments, lovely papers and exquisitely soft brushes have been on sale at Poggi's since 1825.
✉ Via del Gesù 74–5 ☎ 06 678 4477 🕐 Mon–Fri 9–1, 4–7.30, Sat 9–1; ✉ Via Piè di Marmo 40–1 ☎ 06 6830 8014 🕐 Mon–Fri 9–1, 4–7.30, Sat 9–1

RINASCITA

Originally an austere left-wing bookshop; now an excellent and broad-based store with English titles and a linked CD/music shop next door.
✉ Via delle Botteghe Oscure 1–3 ☎ 06 679 7637 🕐 Mon–Fri 9–8, Sat 10–8, Sun 10–2, 4–8

RIZZOLI

Italy's largest bookshop appears dated alongside newer rivals, but you should be able to find most Italian books in print (as well as a selection in English).
✉ Galleria Colonna, Largo Chigi 15 ☎ 06 679 6641 🕐 Mon–Sat 9–7, Sun 10–1.25, 4–7.55

VERTECCHI

The best source of stationery, napkins, wrapping paper, boxes, obelisks and books covered in beautiful Florentine marbled paper.
✉ Via della Croce 70 ☎ 06 679 0155 🕐 Tue–Sat 9.30–7.30, Mon 3.30–7.30; ✉ Via dei Gracchi 179 ☎ 06 321 3559 🕐 Tue–Sat 9.30–7.30, Mon 3.30–7.30

China, Glass & Fabric

BASSETTI

Central shop with a dazzling collection of high-quality Italian silks and other luxurious fabrics, plus everyday materials.

✉ Corso Vittorio Emanuele II 73 ☎ 06 689 2326 ⏰ Tue–Sat 9–7.30 (Jul–Aug 9–1, 4–6), Mon 4–6

CASIMON

This glorious shop sells an enormous variety of objects in marble, stone, glass and semi-precious stones, from ornamental marble balls and bookends to tables and colossal lampshades.

✉ Via della Lungaretta 90 ☎ 06 581 4860 ⏰ Daily 11am–midnight

CULTI

Shop near Piazza Navona packed with linens, well-designed kitchen utensils, plates, glasses, vases, towels, sheets and a host of other articles for the home.

✉ Via della Vetrina 16a ☎ 06 683 2180 ⏰ Tue–Sat 10–1.30, 4–7.30, Mon 4–7.30

FRETTE

This chain is a byword across Italy for the finest towels, sheets and household linens. Prices are high, but the quality is excellent.

✉ Via del Corso 381 ☎ 06 678 6862 ⏰ Tue–Sat 9.40–7.30, Mon 3.30–7.30; ✉ Via Nazionale 80 ☎ 06 488 2641 ⏰ Tue–Sat 9.40–7.30, Mon 3.30–7.30; ✉ Piazza di Spagna 11 ☎ 06 679 0673 ⏰ Tue–Sat 9.40–7.30, Mon 3.30–7.30

GINORI

One of the top Italian names in modern and traditional glass and china.

✉ Via del Tritone 177 ☎ 06 679 3836 ⏰ Tue–Sat 10–7.30

HOUSE & KITCHEN

More traditional than Spazio Sette (see below). This shop sells a full range of household goods, notably a vast selection of kitchen utensils and general kitchenware.

✉ Via del Plebiscito 103 ☎ 06 679 4208 ⏰ Mon–Sat 9.30–8, Sun 10.30–2, 3.30–7.30; closed Sun in Jul and Aug

ORNAMENTUM

A beautiful shop selling silks and other sumptuous fabrics, tassels, brocades and other furnishing accessories.

✉ Via dei Coronari 227 ☎ 06 687 6849 ⏰ Tue–Fri 9–1, 4–7.30, Sat 9–1, Mon 4–7.30; closed Aug

SPAZIO SETTE

On three floors at the splendid Palazzo Lazzaroni are superbly designed objects ranging from candles to clocks and corkscrews.

✉ Via dei Barbieri 7 ☎ 06 6880 4261 ⏰ Tue–Sat 9.30–1, 3.30–7.30, Mon 3.30–7.30

STILVETRO

Italian glassware and china, much of it from Tuscany, make this established shop a good source for authentic and inexpensive gifts.

✉ Via Frattina 56 ☎ 06 679 0258 ⏰ Tue–Sat 9.30–2, 2.30–7.30, Mon 3.30–7.30

GIFTS WITH A TWIST

For a souvenir with a difference, visit the extraordinary shops on Via dei Cestari, just south of the Pantheon, which specialise in all sorts of religious clothes, candles and vestments. Crucifixes, rosaries, statues of saints and other religious souvenirs can be found in shops on Via di Porta Angelica near the Vatican. Alternatively, visit the Farmacia Santa Maria della Scala (✉ Piazza Santa Maria della Scala), an 18th-century monastic pharmacy that sells herbal remedies.

Food & Wine

LOCAL SHOPPING

Roman supermarkets are few and far between (► panel opposite) and most food is still bought in tiny neighbourhood shops known as *alimentari*. Every street of every 'village' or district in the city has one or more of these general shops, a source of everything from olive oil and pasta to candles and corn and bunion treatments. They are also good places to buy picnic provisions—many sell bread and wine—and most have a delicatessen counter that will make you a sandwich (*panino*) from the meats and cheeses on display. For something a little more special, or for food gifts to take home, visit Via della Croce, a street renowned for its wonderful delicatessens.

AI MONASTERI

This unusual, large and rather dark old shop sells the products of seven Italian monasteries, from honeys, wines, natural preserves and liqueurs to herbal cures and elixirs.
✚ G7 ✉ Piazza Cinque Lune 76 ☎ 06 6880 2783
🕐 Fri–Wed 9–1, 4.30–7.30, Thu 9–1; closed 1st week of Sep

ANTICA ENOTECA

A beautiful old-fashioned shop where you can buy wine by the bottle or sip it by the glass amid trickling fountains and marble-topped tables. You can also buy good snacks or light meals.
✚ J5 ✉ Via della Croce 76b
☎ 06 679 0896 🕐 Daily 11am–midnight

CASTRONI

Castroni boasts Rome's largest selection of imported delicacies, a mouthwatering array of Italian specialities and an amazing range of coffees.
✚ E5 ✉ Via Cola di Rienzo 196 ☎ 06 687 4383
🕐 Mon–Sat 8–8

ENOTECA BUCCONE

Rome's most select and best-stocked wine shop occupies a 17th-century coach house. Snacks and light meals are also available in a small room off the main shop.
✚ H4 ✉ Via di Ripetta 19–20
☎ 06 361 2154 🕐 Mon–Sat 9–8.30, closed Aug

ENOTECA AL GOCCETTO

Wines from all over Italy are sold in this old bishop's *palazzo*, complete with original floors and wooden ceiling.
✚ F8 ✉ Via dei Banchi Vecchi 14 ☎ 06 686 4268
🕐 Mon–Sat 11.30–2, 5.30–11, closed 3 weeks in Aug

PASTA ALL'UOVO

An excellent place to purchase fresh or dried pasta in a wide range of bizarre colours and shapes—good souvenirs to take home
✚ J5 ✉ Via della Croce 8
☎ 06 679 3102 🕐 Mon–Sat 8.30–1, 4–8

PIETRO FRANCHI

A rival to nearby Castroni as Rome's best delicatessen. Offers a selection of regional food and wines, and dishes to take out—anything from cold antipasti to succulent roast meats.
✚ E5 ✉ Via Cola di Rienzo 204 ☎ 06 686 4576
🕐 Mon–Sat 8am–9pm

SALUMERIA FOCACCI

For variety and quality this is one of the best in a street renowned for its food shops (*salumeria* means delicatessen; *salumi* are cold cuts).
✚ J5 ✉ Via della Croce 43
☎ 06 679 1228 🕐 Mon–Sat 8.30–7.30

VINCENZO TASCIONI

This most famous of Roman neighbourhood shops sells fresh pasta in over 30 varieties, all made on the premises.
✚ E5 ✉ Via Cola di Rienzo 211 ☎ 06 324 3152
🕐 Mon–Sat 9.30–7.30 (may close 2–2.30 some days)

Street Markets

CAMPO DE' FIORI

This picturesque market is in a pretty, central square. Fruit and vegetables dominate, but you can also buy fish, flowers and beans.

➕ G8 ✉ Piazza Campo de' Fiori 🕓 Mon–Sat 7am–1.30pm

MERCATO ANDREA DORIA

A large, local market that serves the neighbourhood northwest of the Vatican. Stands mostly sell meat, fish, fruit and vegetables, but there are a few with shoes and quality clothes.

➕ B4 ✉ Via Andrea Doria-Via Tunisi 🕓 Mon–Sat 7am–1pm

MERCATO DE' FIORI

Not to be confused with Campo de' Fiori, this wholesale flower market in a covered hall is open to the public only on Tuesdays. Prices are particularly reasonable for cut flowers, potted plants and Mediterranean blooms.

➕ C3 ✉ Via Trionfale 47–9 🕓 Tue 10.30am–1pm

MERCATO DI PIAZZA VITTORIO

Rome's largest and most colourful general market is no longer in this square close to Termini. However, it retains its name, and now fills the streets surrounding its old name.

➕ Q9 ✉ Piazza Vittorio Emanuele II 🕓 Mon–Sat 7am–2pm

MERCATO DELLE STAMPE

Tucked away, about a dozen stands sell old books, magazines and prints (*stampe* in Italian). Be prepared to haggle.

➕ H6 ✉ Largo della Fontanella di Borghese 🕓 Mon–Sat 9–5.30

MERCATO DI VIA SANNIO

This market in the shadow of San Giovanni in Laterano sells bags, belts, shoes, toys and inexpensive clothes. Stands nearby peddle more interesting bric-a-brac and second-hand clothes.

➕ Off map Q11 ✉ Via Sannio 🕓 Mon–Fri 10–1.30, Sat 10–6

PIAZZA COPPELLE

This tiny, attractive local food market is an oasis among the cars and tourists. Close to the Pantheon.

➕ H7 ✉ Piazza Coppelle 🕓 Mon–Sat 7am–1pm

PIAZZA SAN COSIMATO

It is a great shame that few visitors manage to discover what this mid-size general neighbourhood food market in Trastevere has to offer.

➕ F11 ✉ Piazza San Cosimato 🕓 Mon–Sat 7am–1pm

PORTA PORTESE

Everything and anything is for sale at this famous flea market, though the few genuine antiques are highly priced. By mid-morning crowds are huge, so come early and guard your belongings.

➕ Off map G11 ✉ Via Porta Portese-Via Ippolito Nuevo 🕓 Sun 6.30am–2pm

SUPERMARKETS

At the other extreme to Rome's sprawling markets are its handful of supermarkets and department stores, both types of shop that are still rather alien to most Italians. The best department store is La Rinascente, which has a central branch at Via del Corso 189, and another in Piazza Fiume. Coin is also good, though a little less stylish, and is close to San Giovanni in Laterano at Piazzale Appio 15. Cheaper again are the large Upim and Standa chains, which have reasonably priced clothes and general household goods.

Bars by Night

WHAT TO DRINK

The most inexpensive way to drink beer in Italy is from the keg (*alla spina*). Measures are *piccola*, *media* and *grande* (usually 33cl, 50cl and a litre respectively). Foreign canned or bottled beers (*in lattina* or *in bottiglia*) are expensive. Italian brands like Peroni are a little less expensive: a Peroncino (25cl bottle) is a good thirst-quencher. Aperitifs (*aperitivi*) include popular non-alcoholic drinks like Aperol, Crodino and San Pellegrino bitter. A glass of red or white wine is *un bicchiere di vino rosso/bianco*.

BAR DELLA PACE
(► 70)

BEVITORIA
Friendlier and more intimate than most large or touristy bars on Piazza Navona. Primarily a wine bar (the cellar is part of Domitian's former stadium). Gets busy, so arrive early.

➕ G7 ✉ Piazza Navona 72 ☎ 06 6880 1022 🕐 Mon–Sat 11am–1am 🚌 46, 62, 64 to Corso Vittorio Emanuele II or 30, 70, 81, 87, 116 to Corso del Rinascimento

CAVOUR 313
At the Forum end of Via Cavour, this easily missed wine bar has a relaxed, student feel. Good snacks from the bar and wine by the glass or bottle.

➕ N8 ✉ Via Cavour 313 ☎ 06 678 5496 🕐 Mon–Sat 12.30–2.30, 7.30–12.30 (also Sun 7.30–12.30, Oct–May) 🚌 75, 84, 117 to Via Cavour or 84, 85, 87, 175 to Via dei Fori Imperiali

CUL DE SAC
An established informal wine bar near Piazza Navona with pine tables and a big marble bar. More than 1,400 wines, plus first-rate snacks, light meals and cheese and salami from every region in Italy.

➕ G8 ✉ Piazza Pasquino 73 ☎ 06 6880 1094 🕐 Daily noon–4pm, 7–12.30 🚌 46, 62, 64 to Corso Vittorio Emanuele II

DRUID'S DEN
Friendly and realistic Irish pub that appeals to Romans and expats alike. Also try The Fiddler's

Elbow, a popular sister pub around the corner at Via dell'Olmata 43.

➕ N8 ✉ Via San Martino ai Monti 28 ☎ 06 4890 4781 🕐 Mon–Fri 5pm–12.30am, Sat–Sun 4pm–1am 🚇 Cavour 🚌 75, 84, 117 to Via Cavour or 16, 70, 71, 360 to Piazza Santa Maria Maggiore

IL PICCOLO
Intimate wine bar close to Piazza Navona, ideal for a romantic interlude.

➕ G8 ✉ Via del Governo Vecchio 74–5 ☎ 06 6880 1746 🕐 Mon–Fri 11am–2am, Sat–Sun 7pm–2am 🚌 46, 62, 64 to Corso Vittorio Emanuele II

LA VINERIA REGGIO
The quainter side of night-time drinking. Fusty and old-fashioned inside, with characters to match; tables on the city's most evocative square. Also try the popular Drunken Ship pub virtually next door.

➕ G8 ✉ Campo de' Fiori 15 ☎ 06 6880 3268 🕐 Mon–Sat 8.30am–2am, Sun 5pm–2am 🚌 46, 62, 64 to Corso Vittorio Emanuele II or 70, 81, 87 to Corso del Rinascimento

TRASTÈ
(► 70)

TRINITY COLLEGE
English and Irish-style pubs are all the rage—this is one of the better ones. Its serves inexpensive food as well as Guinness and other drinks.

➕ J8 ✉ Via del Collegio Romano ☎ 06 678 6472 🕐 Daily noon–3am 🚌 62, 63, 81, 85, 95, 117, 119 to Via del Corso and all services to Piazza Venezia

Clubs & Discos

AKAB-CAVE

In the Testaccio area, this very popular and long-established club is on two levels (one underground—hence Cave) with a garden area and varied music policy.

✉ Via Monte Testaccio 69
☎ 06 578 2390 🕐 Tue–Sat 11pm–4.30am 🚇 Piramide
🚌 3, 60, 75, 95, 118
💲 Moderate

ALIEN

Decor inspired by the movie of the same name. An up-to-the-minute music policy has turned this futuristic club into one of Rome's nightspots of the moment.

✉ Via Velletri 13–19
☎ 06 841 2212 🕐 Tue–Sun 11pm–4am 🚌 N60 to Piazza Fiume 💲 Inexpensive to expensive (variable)

BLACK OUT

Black Out has gained a well-deserved reputation over the years as one of the best alternative clubs. Music is mainly punk, thrash, Gothic—'dark' in Roman parlance.

✉ Via Saturnia 18 ☎ 06 7049 6791 🕐 Thu–Sat 10.30pm–4am 🚇 Re di Roma
🚌 55N and 87 to Piazza Tuscolo
💲 Inexpensive to moderate (variable)

GILDA

Gilda's louche and languid atmosphere has been attracting stars, VIPs and wannabe socialites for years. Bar, two stylish restaurants, glittering dance floor. Note that men are required to wear a smart jacket.

✉ Via Mario de' Fiori 97
☎ 06 678 4838 🕐 Tue–Sun 11pm–4am 🚇 Spagna
🚌 52, 53, 61, 71, 85, 160, 850 to Piazza San Silvestro
💲 Expensive

L'ALIBI

Primarily a gay disco, but not exclusively, L'Alibi is one of the most reliable (and most established) clubs now mushrooming in trendy Testaccio.

✉ Via Monte Testaccio 40–44
☎ 06 574 3448 🕐 Wed–Sun 11pm–4.30am 🚇 Piramide
🚌 23, 75, 95, 170, 280 to Piazza di Porta San Paolo or Via Monte Testaccio 💲 Moderate

LA SCALA

La Scala is one of the most popular bars and clubs in Trastevere. Loud, lively and young, it offers wine, beer, some food (snacks and light meals) and occasional live music. There are a few outside tables.

✉ Via della Scala 4
☎ 06 580 3610 🕐 Daily 4pm–2am or later 🚌 H, 8, 780 to Piazza Sidney Sonnino or 23, 280 to Lungarno Sanzio
💲 Free

PIPER

Open since the 1960s, Piper is consistently popular, thanks partly to its programme of constant updating and refurbishment.

✉ Via Tagliamento 9
☎ 06 855 5398 or 06 841 4459 🕐 Hours erratic. Sat and Sun only in winter 🚌 63, 86, 92, N29, N30 to Via Tagliamento
💲 Very expensive

Opera & Classical Music

CHURCH MUSIC

Following a decree from Pope John Paul II, all concert programmes in Roman churches currently have a marked religious bias. Music can range from small-scale organ recitals to full-blown choirs and orchestras. Be on the lookout for posters advertising concerts outside churches and around the city. The Coro della Cappella Giulia sings at 10.30am and 5pm on Sundays in St. Peter's. Sant' Ignazio di Loyola, San Paolo entro le Mura, San Nicola in Carcere, San Marcello al Corso and Santa Maria dell'Orto are churches that regularly host choral and organ recitals.

ACCADEMIA FILARMONICA ROMANA

Founded in 1821, the Roman Philharmonic Academy numbers Rossini, Verdi and Donizetti among its distinguished early luminaries. It does not support its own choir or orchestra, but presents high-quality recitals of contemporary, choral and symphonic music by well-known national and international performers. Concerts are held at the Sala Casella or the nearby Teatro Olimpico (➤ 83).
✉ Via Flaminia 118 ☎ 06 320 1752; www.filarmonicaroma.org
🎵 Concerts Thu (also occasionally Tue), mid-Oct to mid-May; Box Office: daily 9am–1pm, 6–7pm; Information daily 3–7pm
🚍 2, 48, 200, 201, 220, 910 to Piazza Antonio Mancini

ACCADEMIA NAZIONALE DI SANTA CECILIA

In existence since the 16th century, Rome's main classical music body stages concerts by its own orchestra and choir, and organizes recitals and concerts by visiting choirs and orchestras. Most events are held at the Auditorio Pio (➤ this page). Outdoor recitals and ballet performances are held in summer in a variety of outdoor locations.
✉ Via Vittoria 6 ☎ Tickets 06 6880 1044; www.santacecilia.it

ACQUARIO ROMANO

An innovative organization whose concerts showcase contemporary classical music—both well-known and, occasionally, more obscure.
✉ Piazza Manfredo Fanti 47 ☎ 06 446 8616 or 06 6880 9222 🚇 Termini or Vittorio Emanuele 🚍 4, 9, 70, 71

ASSOCIAZIONE IL TEMPIETTO

Organizes summer concerts held outdoors most nights in the Teatro di Marcello: usually involving younger and less experienced musicians. Concerts are also held the rest of the year in a variety of venues.
✉ Via del Teatro di Marcello 44 ☎ 06 8713 1590; www.tempietto.com 🚍 44, 63, 81, 95, and services to Piazza Venezia

ASSOCIAZIONE MUSICALE ROMANA

Stages a summer season of chamber recitals at a number of venues, including the French Academy in the Villa Medici.
✉ Via dei Banchi Vecchi 61 ☎ 06 686 8441 or 06 3936 6322

AUDITORIO PIO (AUDITORIO DI SANTA CECILIA)

✉ Via della Conciliazione 4 Box office ☎ 06 6880 1044 🎵 Mon–Fri 10.30–1.30, 3–6 🚍 64 to Porta Cavellegger or 23, 34, 40, 46, 62, 64, 98, 280 to Ponte Vittorio Emanuelle II

AULA MAGNA DELL'UNIVERSITÀ LA SAPIENZA

✉ Piazzale Aldo Moro 5 ☎ 06 361 0051 🎵 Concerts Tue 8.30pm, Sat

5.30pm, Oct–May 🚌 310, 649 to Viale dell'Università

IL GONFALONE

A small but prestigious company that hosts chamber music and other small-scale recitals.
✉ Oratorio del Gonfalone, Via del Gonfalone 32a
Information ✉ Vicolo della Scimmia 1b ☎ 06 687 5952
🕐 Concerts Thu 9pm, Oct–Jun; Box office Mon–Fri 9am–1pm, day of concert 9am–9pm
🚌 46, 62, 64 to Corso Vittorio Emanuele II or 23, 116, 280 to Lungotevere di Sangallo

ISTITUTO UNIVERSITARIO DEI CONCERTI (IUC)

The IUC students keep the music exciting and eclectic. Concert cycles are devoted to the music and composers of a different country each year. Most recitals are in the university's Aula Magna (► 82) east of Stazione Termini.
✉ Lungotevere Flaminio 50 ☎ 06 361 0051/0052;
www.concertiive.it
🕐 Box office Mon–Fri 10am–1pm, 3–6pm, Sat 10am–1pm 🚌 225 to Piazza Mancini

PARCO DELLA MUSICA

This magnificent new Renzo Piano-designed centre has three performance spaces (including one outdoors), and has quickly become one of the city's premier venues for classical and other concerts.
✉ Viale Pietro De Coubertin 15 ☎ 06 8069 2492;
www.musicaperroma.it

🚌 53, 217, 910 to Viale Pietro De Coubertin

ROMAEUROPA FESTIVAL

This festival in late summer showcases contemporary European music (plus art and other culture) and is organized by the French, German and other Rome-based international academies. Some performances are in the gardens of the Villa Medici.
✉ Via XX Settembre 3 ☎ 06 4890 4024;
www.romeeuropa.net

TEATRO COSTANZ (DELL'OPERA)

Rome's opera house is enduring lean times. Crippled by dwindling finances, the reputation of its orchestra and choir and the quality of performances has diminished. Austerity has forced a concentration on the mainstream repertoire. Mid-June and mid-August operas are staged outdoors at venues, which change from year to year.
✉ **Opera** Piazza Beniamo Gigli ☎ 06 481 7003;
www.opera.roma.it
Box office ✉ Via Firenze 72 ☎ 06 481601 or Hello Tickets 06 808 8352 🕐 Opera mid-Jun to mid-Aug, Dec–May; Recitals Nov–Jun 🚇 Termini 🚌 H, 40, 60, 64, 70, 71, 170 to Via Nazionale or services to Termini

TEATRO OLIMPICO

✉ Piazza Gentile da Fabriano ☎ 06 323 4890
Box Office ☎ 06 326 5991 🕐 Daily 11–7 🚌 225 Piazza Mancini

MUSIC OUTDOORS

Alfresco recitals often take place in the cloisters of Santa Maria della Pace in July (part of the Serenate in Chiostro season); in the Villa Doria Pamphilj in July (as part of the the Festival Villa Pamphilj); in the grounds of the Villa Giulia in the summer (as part of the Stagione Estivi dell'Orchestra dell'Accademia di Santa Cecilia); and in the Area Archeologica del Teatro di Marcello from July to September (as part of the Estate al Tempietto, also known as the Concerti del Tempietto). Note that the venues may change from year to year.

83

Live Music

LISTINGS AND TICKETS

For details of forthcoming events consult the listings magazine *Romac'è* (www.romace.it), available from most newsstands, or the free *Trovaroma* listings supplement published with the Thursday edition of *La Repubblica*. Otherwise, see the daily listings of *Il Messaggero*. Tickets for events can be bought at the door or from Orbis (✉ Piazza Esquilino 37 ☎ 06 474 4776 ④ Mon–Sat 9.30–1, 4–7.30). Note that the agency does not accept credit cards. Tickets are also available from the Ricordi music shop (✉ Via Cesare Battisti 120 ☎ 06 679 8022 ④ Mon–Sat 9–7.30, Sun 3.30–7.30). As with clubs and discos (► 81), you may need to buy an annual membership card (*una tessara*) on top of a ticket for a music venue. Virtually all clubs close between late July and early September.

ALEXANDERPLATZ

A restaurant and cocktail bar north of St. Peter's with live jazz.
✉ Via Ostia 9 ☎ 06 3974 2171 ④ Mon–Sat 9–2, Sep–Jun ⊕ Ottaviano
🚌 29N, 30N, 99N and 23, 70, 490, 913, 991, 994, 999 to Largo Trionfale-Viale delle Milizie 🎫 Four-month membership (expensive); usually free to tourists on production of passport

BIG MAMA

Rome's best blues club; also hosts rock and jazz.
✉ Vicolo San Francesco a Ripa 18 ☎ 06 581 2551; www.bigmama.it ④ Daily 9pm–1.30am, Oct–Jun 🚌 H, 8, 780 to Viale di Trastevere 🎫 Yearly membership (moderate) plus fee for some concerts

CAFFÈ LATINO

The oldest club in Testaccio, devoted to eating, drinking, live music and dance sessions. Mostly jazz, but rap, blues and other genres are here.
✉ Via Monte Testaccio 96 ☎ 06 5728 8556 ④ Tue–Thu, Sun 10.30pm–2.30am, Fri, Sat 10.30pm–4.30am, Sep–Jul ⊕ Piramide 🚌 3, 23, 30, 75, 280, 716 to Via Marmorata 🎫 Yearly membership (expensive)

CONTROLOCALE

About five minutes' walk from the Colosseum, this live jazz and blues club also serves light meals.
✉ Via di San Giovanni in Laterano 142 ☎ 06 700 9844 ④ Daily 10:30am–3pm
🚌 85, 117, 850 to Via di San Giovanni in Laterano or services to Piazza del Colosseo 🎫 Moderate

FONCLEA

Jazz predominates at this bar, restaurant and club close to St. Peter's.
✉ Via Crescenzio 82a ☎ 06 689 6302 ④ Mon–Thu, Sun 8pm–2am, Fri, Sat 9pm–3am ⊕ Ottaviano 🚌 29N, 30N, and 23, 34, 49, 492, 990 to Via Crescenzio 🎫 Free except Sat (inexpensive)

GREGORY'S

A relaxed club close to the Spanish Steps and one of the few places in central Rome where you can listen to jazz.
✉ Via Gregoriana 54/a ☎ 06 679 6386; www.gregorysjazzclub.it ④ Tue–Sun 5.30pm–2/3.30am 🚌 119 to Piazza di Spagna 🎫 Variable

NEW MISSISSIPPI JAZZ CLUB

Re-creates the feel of an American jazz dive with period photos of past performers on the walls. The biggest names play on Friday and Saturday. Food available.
✉ Borgo Angelico 18a ☎ 06 6880 6348 ④ Mon–Fri 9.30pm–2am ⊕ Ottaviano 🎫 Membership (inexpensive)

RIPARTE CAFÉ

Modern and stylish, this is a popular nightspot; so be sure to reserve ahead, particularly if you want eat here. It also has live performers in a variety of styles most evenings.
✉ Via Orti di Trastevere 7 ☎ 06 586 1816 ④ Tue–Sat 8pm–1am 🚌 8, 780 🎫 Expensive

Sport

HORSE RACING

IPPODROMO DELLE CAPANNELLE

Rome's main race course hosts flat racing, steeplechasing and trotting.

✉ Via Appia Nuova 1255
☎ 06 718 8750
🕐 Races: usually Tue, Fri and Sun from 2.30, Sep–Jun
🚌 650, 671 to Via Appia Nuova

FOOTBALL

STADIO OLIMPICO

Home to Rome's two big football (soccer) teams, AS Roma and Lazio. Games are played here on alternate Sundays.

✉ Viale dei Gladiatori
☎ 06 3685 7520 🚌 32, 48, 69, 220, 224, 232, 280, 911 to Lungotevere Maresciallo Cadorna
Ticket office
☎ 06 323 7333
🕐 Daily 9–1.30, 2.30–6
AS Roma information
☎ 06 06 678 6514 or 06 6920 0642; www.asromacalcio.it
Lazio information
☎ 06 3685 7566/06 482 6768; www.sslazio.it

GOLF

COUNTRY CLUB CASTEL-GANDOLFO

An 18-hole course designed by Robert Trent Jones.

✉ Via Santo Spirito 13, Pavona Laghetto ☎ 06 931 2301
🕐 Daily 8–8 🚉 Termini to Pavona, then taxi

SPECTATOR SPORTS

FORO ITALICO

One of the world's finest sports stadia when built in the 1930s, the Foro Italico is today best known as the site of the Italian open tennis tournament in May.

✉ Lungotevere Maresciallo Diaz-Viale dei Gladiatori 31
☎ 06 36851 or 06 333 6316 or 06 3685 8218 🚌 280 to Lungotevere Maresciallo Cadorna

PALAZZETTO DELLO SPORT

Part of the EUR complex built for the 1960 Olympic Games. Hosts boxing, fencing, tennis and wrestling.

✉ Piazza Apollodoro-Via Flaminia 🕐 Daily 7am–8pm
🚇 Flaminio 🚌 225, 910 to Piazza Apollodoro

PALAZZO DELLO SPORT

Another part of the EUR complex, this stadium hosts indoor games, most notably basketball, usually on winter weekends.

✉ Via dell'Umanesimo ☎ 06 592 5006 🚇 EUR Palasport

SWIMMING

Public swimming pools in Rome are either some way from the centre or not terribly pleasant. Your best option is to use a hotel pool; many open to non-residents for a daily fee. Two of the best are at the Aldrovandi Palace and Cavalieri Hilton.

Aldrovandi Palace
✉ Via Ulisse Aldrovandi 15
☎ 06 322 3993
🕐 Daily 10–6, Jun–Sep
🚌 19, 30 to Via Aldrovandi
Cavalieri Hilton
✉ Via Alberto Cadlolo 101
☎ 06 35091 or 06 3509 2950
🚌 907, 913, 991, 999 to Via Medaglie d'Oro

LOCAL RIVALRY

Rivalry between Rome's two Serie A (first division) football (soccer) teams is intense. Lazio, a traditional underachiever, is currently doing as well as AS Roma. Both teams have won the championship or *scudetto* in present years. AS Roma is known as the *giallorossi* (after the team's red and yellow uniform), while Lazio players sport the nickname *biancocelesti*, referring to their colours, white and sky blue. The team symbols—AS Roma's wolf cub and Lazio's eagle—are often seen among city graffiti.

85

Luxury Hotels

HOTEL PRICES

Expect to pay the following prices per night for the least expensive double room, but it's always worth asking when you make your reservation whether special deals are available.

Budget   up to €100

Mid-range up to €200

Luxury   from €200

Hotels are classified by the Italian state into five categories from one star (basic) to five stars (luxury). The prices each can charge are set by law and must be displayed in the room (you will usually find them on the door). However, prices within a hotel can vary from room to room (and some hotels have off- and peak-season rates). If a room is too expensive, do not be afraid to ask for a less expensive one. Watch for extras like air-conditioning and obligatory breakfasts. Single rooms cost about two-thirds the price of doubles, and to have an extra bed in a room adds 35 per cent to the bill.

ALBERGO DEL SOLE AL PANTHEON

Chic and old—open since 1467. Opposite the Pantheon; if you can stand the crowds, the location is one of the best. 25 rooms.
➕ H7 ✉ Piazza della Rotonda 63 ☎ 06 678 0441; fax 06 6994 0689; www.hotelsolealpantheon.com
🚌 119 to Piazza della Rotonda or 70, 81, 87 to Corso del Rinascimento

AMBASCIATORI PALACE

One of the more venerable and stately of Via Veneto's large luxury hotels, with a traditional feel and opulent appearance. 110 rooms
➕ M5 ✉ Via Vittorio Veneto 62 ☎ 06 47493; fax 06 474 3601; www.ambasciatoripalace.com
Ⓜ Barberini 🚌 52, 53, 95, 116, 119 to Via Vittorio Veneto

DE RUSSIE

A glorious hotel just off Piazza del Popolo distinguished by its modern and stylish design. The 94 rooms are calm and bright, and most have views of the delightful gardens, a lovely spot to dine al fresco in summer.
➕ D4 ✉ Via del Babuino 9 ☎ 06 328 881; fax 3288 8888; www.roccofortehotels.com
Ⓜ Flaminio 🚌 117, 119 to Piazza del Popolo

EXCELSIOR

Large and grand: Everything is on an enormous scale, from the vast silk rugs to the 320 palatial bedrooms (35 suites).
➕ M5 ✉ Via Vittorio Veneto 125 ☎ 06 47081; fax 06 482 6205; www.westin.com

Ⓜ Barberini 🚌 52, 53, 95, 116, 119 to Via Vittorio Veneto

HASSLER-VILLA MEDIOI

Well located longtime jet-set and VIP haunt, just above the Spanish Steps. 100 rooms.
➕ K5 ✉ Piazza Trinità dei Monti 6 ☎ 06 699 340; fax 06 678 9991; www.hotelhasslerroma.com
Ⓜ Spagna 🚌 119 to Piazza di Spagna

ST. REGIS GRAND

Not in the most salubrious location, but immensely lavish and luxurious. 134 rooms, plus 35 suites.
➕ N6 ✉ Via Vittorio Emanuele Orlando 3 ☎ 06 47091/ 474709; fax 06 474 7307; www.stregis.com Ⓜ Repubblica
🚌 H, 40, 170, 492, 910 to Piazza della Repubblica

LORD BYRON

Small, refined and extremely chic, away from the centre in leafy Parioli. Noted for its excellent restaurant Relais Le Jardin. 28 rooms, plus 9 suites.
➕ J1 ✉ Via Giuseppe de Notaris 5 ☎ 06 322 0404; fax 06 322 0405; www.lordbyronhotel.com
Ⓜ Flaminio 🚌 52 to Via Buozzi

RAPHAEL

Intimate, charming and ivy covered—hidden away yet near Piazza Navona. The 73 rooms are a little small but immaculate. Reserve ahead.
➕ G7 ✉ Largo Febo 2 ☎ 06 682831; fax 06 687 8993; www.raphaelhotel.com 🚌 70, 81, 87 to Corso del Rinasciment

Mid-Range Hotels

CAMPO DE' FIORI
Good value, close to
Campo de' Fiori. The 27
rooms are small but pretty
and there is a roof garden.
🕂 G8 ✉ Via del Biscione 6
☎ 06 6880 6865; fax 06 687
6003 🚌 46, 62, 64 to Corso
Vittorio Emanuele II

CESARI
A friendly, no-frills hotel
with a loyal clientele.
Perfectly located between
the Corso and the
Pantheon. 47 rooms.
🕂 J7 ✉ Via di Pietra 89a
☎ 06 674 9701; fax 06 6749
7030 🚌 60, 62, 85, 117, 119,
160 to Via del Corso

COLUMBUS
A converted monastery
very close to St. Peter's. A
favourite with visiting
cardinals. 92 rooms.
🕂 G7 ✉ Via della
Conciliazione 33 ☎ 06 686
5435; fax 06 686 4874;
www.hotelcolumbus.net 🚌 23,
34 to Via della Conciliazione or 64
to Piazza San Pietro

DUE TORRI
Hidden in a tiny alley
between Piazza Navona
and the Tiber. The 26
rooms vary from stylish to
plain, but all are adequate.
🕂 H6 ✉ Vicolo del Leonetto
23–5 ☎ 06 687 6983;
fax 06 685 5442;
www.hotelduetorriroma.com
🚌 30, 70, 81, 87, 116, 186 to
Corso del Rinascimento or
Lungotevere Marzio

HOTEL PORTOGHESI
A well-known if slightly
fading hotel with a roof
terrace. In a cobbled street
north of Sant' Agostino
and Piazza Navona.

22 rooms, plus 5 suites.
🕂 H7 ✉ Via dei Portoghesi 1
☎ 06 686 4231; fax 06 687
6976 🚌 30, 70, 81, 87, 116 to
Corso del Rinascimento

LA RESIDENZA
A good choice, close to Via
Vittorio Veneto and
reasonably priced. Stylish
public spaces, 26 spacious
and comfortable rooms.
Terrace and roof garden.
🕂 L5 ✉ Via Emilia 22–4
☎ 06 488 0789; fax 06
485721 Ⓜ Barberini
🚌 52, 53, 80, 95, 116, 119
to Via Vittorio Veneto

LOCARNO
In a quietish side street
close to Piazza del Popolo.
Much genuine 1920s art-
nouveau decor. 46 rooms.
🕂 H4 ✉ Via della Penna 22
☎ 06 361 0841; fax 06 321
5249; www.hotellocarno.com
Ⓜ Flaminio 🚌 926 to Via di
Ripetta, or 81 to Lungotevere in
Augusta

MANFREDI
Quiet family-run hotel
with 18 pretty rooms, in a
cobbled street of galleries
and antique shops.
🕂 J4 ✉ Via Margutta 61
☎ 06 320 7676; fax 06 320
7736; www.hmanfredi.com
Ⓜ Spagna 🚌 119 to Piazza di
Spagna

SISTINA
Small, efficient and close
to the Piazza di Spagna.
Lovely terrace for drinks
and breakfasts. 23 rooms.
🕂 K6 ✉ Via Sistina 136
☎ 06 474 4176; fax 06 481
8867 Ⓜ Spagna or Barberini
🚌 119 to Piazza di Spagna or
52, 53, 61, 62, 80, 95, 116, 119,
175 to Piazza Barberini

**ACCOMMODATION
AGENCIES**

Two good sources for all kinds
of accommodation, from
hotels to bed-and-breakfast in
all price ranges, are the Hotel
Reservation Agency
(☎ 06 699 1000;
www.hotelreservation.it) and
the website www.romeguide.it

RESERVATIONS

Rome's peak season runs from
Easter to October, but the
city's hotels (in all categories)
are almost invariably busy.
Telephone, write or fax well in
advance to reserve a room
(most receptionists speak
some English, French or
German). Leave a credit card
number or send an
international money order for
the first night's stay to be
certain of the booking.
Reconfirm a few days before
your trip. If you arrive without
a reservation then get to a
hotel early in the morning; by
afternoon most vacated rooms
will have been snapped up.
Don't accept rooms from touts
at Stazione Termini.

Budget Accommodation

NOISE

Noise is a fact of life in every Roman hotel, whatever the price category. Surveys have shown Rome to be the noisiest city in Europe. It is difficult to escape the cacophony entirely (unless the hotel is air-conditioned and windows are double-glazed), but to lessen the potential racket you should avoid rooms overlooking main thoroughfares and the area around Termini in favour of rooms looking out on parks or obscure back streets. Also ask for rooms away from the front of the hotel or facing on to a central courtyard (*cortile*).

ABRUZZI

Twenty-five large rooms (and eight shared bathrooms), some with a view of the Pantheon; rooms at the rear are quieter.
✚ H7 ✉ Piazza della Rotonda 69 ☎ 06 679 2021; fax 06 6978 8076; www.hotelabruzzi.it 🚌 119 to Piazza della Rotonda or 46, 62, 63, 64, 70, 81, 87, 186 to Largo di Torre Argentina

DELLA LUNETTA

A plain 35-room hotel; it lacks panache but makes up for it with its postion just off Campo de' Fiori.
✚ C6 ✉ Piazza del Paradiso ☎ 06 686 1080; fax 06 689 2028 🚌 40, 64 and other services to Corso Vittorio Emanuele II

HOTEL TRASTEVERE

One of only a few hotels in the Trastevere quarter. Nine good, bright rooms, all with private bathrooms, plus 4 apartments.
✚ F11 ✉ Via Luciano Manara 24 ☎ 06 581 4713; fax 06 588 1016 🚌 H, 8, 780 to Piazza S. Sonnino or Viale Trastevere

KATTY

Less grim than most of the countless inexpensive hotels in the unsavoury area near Rome's train station. Always reserve in advance; 28 rooms.
✚ P5 ✉ Via Palestro 5 ☎ 06 444 1216; fax 06 444 1216 🚇 Termini 🚌 64, 65, 170 and all other services to Termini

NAVONA

Twenty-six simple rooms, friendly owners and a superb central location. Reserve well in advance.
✚ H8 ✉ Via dei Sediari 8 ☎ 06 686 4203; fax 06 6880 3802; www.hotelnavona.com 🚌 30, 70, 81, 87, 116, 186 to Corso del Rinascimento

PERUGIA

Little-known, quiet and well located between Via Cavour and the Colosseum. All eight doubles have private bathrooms.
✚ L9 ✉ Via del Colosseo 7 ☎ 06 679 7200; fax 06 678 4635 🚌 75, 84, 117 to Via Cavour or 75, 85, 87, 117, 175 to the Colosseum

POMEZIA

In the city centre close to Campo de' Fiori with 24 small rooms (11 have private bathrooms). Roof terrace and small bar.
✚ H9 ✉ Via dei Chiavari 12 ☎ 06 686 1371; fax 06 686 1371 🚌 46, 62, 64 to Corso Vittorio Emanuele II or 8, 46, 62, 63, 64, 70, 80 to Largo di Torre Argentina

SMERALDO

Thirty-five plain and clean rooms. In a back street close to Campo de' Fiori.
✚ H9 ✉ Vicolo dei Chiodaroli 11 ☎ 06 687 5929; fax 06 6880 5495; www.hotelsmeraldoroma.com 🚌 46, 62, 64 to Corso Vittorio Emanuele II or 8, 46, 62, 63, 64, 70, 80 to Largo di Torre Argentina

SOLE

A popular choice on the edge of Campo de' Fiori. Small garden terrace. 59 rooms.
✚ G8 ✉ Via del Biscione 76 ☎ 06 6880 6873; fax 06 689 3787; www.solealbiscione.it 🚌 46, 62, 64 to Corso Vittorio Emanuele II or 8, 46, 62, 63, 64, 70, 80 to Largo di Torre Argentina

ROME
travel facts

ESSENTIAL FACTS

Electricity

- Current is 220 volts AC, 50 cycles; plugs are the two-round-pin type.

Etiquette

- Do not wear shorts, short skirts or skimpy tops in churches.
- Avoid entering churches while services are in progress.
- Many churches and galleries forbid flash photography or ban photography altogether. Always ask before taking pictures.
- Smoking is common in bars and restaurants, but is banned on public transport.
- Public drunkenness is rare and frowned upon.

Money matters

- Most major traveller's cheques can be changed at banks, though lines can be long.
- Credit cards (*carte di credito*) are gaining in popularity, but cash is preferred. Cash machines are becoming more common.

National holidays

- 1 Jan: New Year's Day
- 6 Jan: Epiphany
- Easter Monday
- 25 Apr: National holiday
- 1 May: Labour Day
- 29 Jun: St. Peter & St. Paul's Day
- 15 Aug: Assumption
- 1 Nov: All Saints' Day
- 8 Dec: Immaculate Conception
- 25 Dec: Christmas Day
- 26 Dec: St. Stephen's Day

Opening hours

- Shops: Tue–Sat 8–1, 4–8, Mon 4–8 (with slight seasonal variations) or, increasingly Mon/Tue–Sat 9.30–7.30. Food shops open on Monday mornings but usually close on Thursday afternoons.
- Restaurants: daily 12.30–3, 7.30–10.30. Many close on Sunday evenings and half- or all day Monday. Most bars and restaurants also have a statutory closing day (*riposo settimanale*) and many close for much of August.
- Churches: variable, but usually daily 7–noon, 4.30–7.
- Museums and galleries: vary considerably; usually close on Monday.
- Banks: Mon–Fri 8.30–1.30. Major branches may also open 3–4 and Saturday morning.
- Post offices: Mon–Fri 8.15 or 9–2; Sat 8.15 or 9–noon or 2.

Tourist information

- Ente Provinciale per il Turismo di Roma ⊠ Via Parigi 11 ☎ 06 3600 4399; www.romaturismo.it ⊕ Mon–Fri 8.15am–7.15pm
- Tourist information kiosks are at:
  - ⊠ Largo Goldoni ☎ 06 6813 6061
  - ⊠ Fori Imperiali ☎ 06 6992 4307
  - ⊠ Piazza delle Cinque Lune ☎ 06 6880 9240
  - ⊠ Via Nazionale ☎ 06 4782 4525
  - ⊠ Piazza San Giovanni in Laterano ☎ 06 7720 3535
  - ⊠ Lungotevere Castel Saint'Angelo-Piazza Pia ☎ 06 6880 9707

PUBLIC TRANSPORT

Buses & trams

- ATAC 🚌 F5 ⊠ Piazza dei Cinquecento ☎ 800 431784 (free-phone) or 06 46951 or 06 57531; www.atac.roma.it ⊕ Mon–Fri 9–1, 2–5 🚇 Termini
- Remember to enter buses by back doors and to leave by centre doors (if you have a pass or validated ticket with unexpired time you can also use the front doors).
- Buy several tickets at once as

some outlets close early.
- There are large fines if you are caught without a ticket.
- Daytime services: 5.30am–11.30pm, depending on the route. Bus stops (*fermate*) list routes and bus numbers. Note that one-way streets often force buses to return along slightly different routes.
- Useful services:
  23 Piazza del Risorgimento (for the Vatican Museums)–Trastevere–Piramide
  75 Termini–Roman Forum–Colosseum–Piramide
  40, 64 Termini–Piazza Venezia–close to Piazza San Pietro/St. Peter's
  110 Sightseeing service from Stazione Termini and other key monuments
  81 Piazza del Risorgimento (Vatican Museums)–Piazza Venezia–Roman Forum–Colosseum
  117, 119 Circular minibus service in the historic centre: Piazza Augusto Imperatore–Piazza della Rotonda (Pantheon)–Via del Corso–Piazza di Spagna
  780 Piazza Venezia–Trastevere

Taxis

- Calling a taxi: the company will give you a taxi code name, a number and the time it will take to get to you. The meter starts running as soon as they are called. Companies include:
  Cosmos Radio Taxis ☎ 06 88177
  Autoradio Taxi ☎ 06 3570
  Capitale Radio ☎ 06 4994
- The minimum fare is valid for 3km (2.5 miles) or the first 9 minutes of a ride. Surcharges are levied between 10pm and 7am, all day Sunday, on national holidays, for airport trips and for each piece of luggage in the boot (trunk).

- Ranks are available in the centre at Termini, Piazza S Sonnino, Pantheon, Piazza di Spagna and Piazza San Silvestro.

For further information on public transport ► 6–7.

MEDIA & COMMUNICATIONS

Newspapers & magazines

- Most Romans read the Rome-based *Il Messaggero*, the mainstream and authoritative *Corriere della Sera* or the centre-left and popularist *La Repubblica* (which has a special Rome edition). Sports papers and news magazines (like *Panorama* and *L'Espresso*) are also popular.
- Foreign newspapers can usually be bought after about 2.30pm on the day of issue from booths (*edicole*) on and close to Termini, Piazza Colonna, Largo di Torre Argentina, Piazza Navona, Via Vittoria Veneto and close to several other tourist sights. European editions of the *International Herald Tribune*, *USA Today* and the *Financial Times* are also available.

Postal service

- Stamps (*francobolli*) can be bought from post offices and tobacconists.
- Post boxes are red and have two slots, one for Rome (marked *Per La Città*) and one for other destinations (*Per Tutte Le Altre Destinazioni*). New boxes, usually blue, are for the quicker priority mail service, or Posta Prioritoria.
- Vatican post can be posted only in the Vatican's blue *Poste Vaticane* post boxes. The Vatican postal service is quicker (although tariffs are the same), but stamps can be bought only at the post offices in the Vatican Museums ⏺ Mon–Fri 8.30am–7pm and in Piazza San

91

Pietro ☎ 06 6988 3406 ⏰ Mon–Fri
8.30am–7pm; Sat 8.30am–6pm
- Main post office (*Ufficio Postale
  Centrale*) ✉ Piazza San Silvestro 18–20
  ☎ 06 678 0788 ⏰ Mon–Fri
  8.30am–6.30/7.30pm, Sat 8.30–1 (9–noon last Sat
  of month)

Telephones

- Telephone numbers listed in this
  book include the Rome area code
  (06), which must be dialled even if
  you are calling from within the city.
- Public telephones are indicated
  by a red or yellow sign showing a
  telephone dial and receiver. They
  are found on the street, in bars
  and restaurants and in special
  offices (*Centri Telefoni*) equipped
  with banks of phones.
- A few *Centri Telefoni* have phones
  that allow you to speak first and
  pay later, but most phones at
  booths require pre-payment.
- Phones usually accept phone
  cards (*schede telefoniche*) available
  from post offices, tobacconists and
  some bars in €2.5, €5 and €7.5
  denominations). Break off the
  card's marked corner before use.
- Cheap rate for calls is Mon–Sat
  10pm–8am and all day Sunday.
- To call Italy from the UK, dial 00
  44 and for the US or Canada dial
  011, followed by 39 (the country
  code for Italy) then the number,
  including the relevant city code.

EMERGENCIES

Lost property

- To make a claim on lost or stolen
  property report the loss to a
  police station, which will issue a
  signed declaration (*una denuncia*)
  for your insurance company. The
  central police station is the
  Questura

✉ Via San Vitale 15 (off Via Nazionale)
☎ 06 46861 (tourist department); 06 4686
2102 🚇 Repubblica
- ATAC lost property
  ✉ Via Nicola Bettoni 1 ☎ 06 581 6040
  ⏰ Mon–Tue, Thu 8.30–1, Wed and Fri
  2.30–5.30
- Metro lost property
  ☎ Line A 06 487 4309; Line B 06 5735 2264
  ⏰ Mon, Wed, Fri 9am–noon
- COTRAL lost property
  ✉ Inquire at the route's origin or telephone
  ☎ 06 57531 or 06 591 5551
- Railway lost property
  ✉ Stazione Termini, Via Giovanni Giolitti 24
  (near Platform 24) ☎ 06 4782 5543
  ⏰ Mon–Fri 7am–10pm/midnight

Medical & dental treatment

- There are emergency rooms
  (*Pronto Soccorso*) at these centres:
  Ospedale Fatebenefratelli
  ✉ Isola Tiberina ☎ 06 683 7299
  Policlinico Umberto
  ✉ Viale Policlinico 155 ☎ 06 446 2341
- The George Eastman Clinic
  provides an emergency dentist
  service. No credit cards.
  ✉ Viale Regina Elena 287/b ☎ 06 844831
- Pharmacies are indicated by a
  large green cross. Opening times
  are usually Mon–Sat 8.30–1, 4–8,
  but a rotating schedule (displayed
  on pharmacy doors) ensures at
  least one pharmacy is open 24
  hours a day, seven days a week.
- The most central English-speaking pharmacist is Internazionale
  ✉ Piazza Barberini 49 ☎ 06 487 1195

Sensible precautions

- Carry all valuables in a belt or
  pouch—never in your pocket.
- Hold bags and cameras across
  your front, never over one shoulder, where they can be grabbed.
- Leave valuables (especially chains
  and earrings) in the hotel safe.
- Beware of persistent gangs of street

children. If approached, hang on to possessions and raise your voice.

- Never leave luggage or other possessions in parked cars.
- Beware of pickpockets, especially in crowded tourist areas, busy shopping streets and buses (the 64 bus to St. Peter's is notorious).
- Avoid parks and the back streets around Termini late at night.
- Women travellers should be prepared for some hassle (rarely threatening) from Italian men.

Telephone numbers

- Police, Fire and Ambulance (general SOS) ☎ 113
- Police (Carabinieri) ☎ 112
- Central Police ☎ 06 46861
- UK Embassy ☎ 06 4220 0001
- US Embassy ☎ 06 46741
- Information ☎ 12
- International information (Europe) ☎ 15
- International information (rest of the world) ☎ 170
- ACI Auto Assistance (car breakdowns) ☎ 116

LANGUAGE

- All Italian words are pronounced as written, with each vowel and consonant sounded. Only the letter *h* is silent, but it modifies the sound of other letters. The letter *c* is hard, as in English 'cat', except when followed by *i* or *e*, when it becomes the soft *ch* of 'cello'. Similarly, *g* is soft (as in the English 'giant') when followed by *i* or *e*—*giardino*, *gelati*; otherwise hard (as in 'gas')—*gatto*. Words ending in *o* are almost always masculine in gender (plural: -*i*); those ending in *a* are generally feminine (plural: -*e*).
- Use the polite second person (*lei*) to speak to strangers and the informal second person (*tu*) to friends or children.

Courtesies

good morning	buon giorno
good afternoon/ good evening	buona sera
good night	buona notte
hello/goodbye (informal)	ciao
hello (on the telephone)	pronto
please	per favore
thank you (very much)	grazie (mille)
you're welcome	prego
how are you? (polite/informal)	come sta/stai?
I'm fine	sto bene
I'm sorry	mi dispiace
excuse me/ I beg your pardon	mi scusi/ permesso

Basic vocabulary

yes/no	sì/no
I do not understand	non ho capito
left/right	sinistra/destra
open/closed	aperto/chiuso
good/bad	buono/cattivo
big/small	grande/piccolo
with/without	con/senza
more/less	più/meno
near/far	vicino/lontano
hot/cold	caldo/freddo
early/late	presto/ritardo
now/later	adesso/più tardi
today/tomorrow	oggi/domani
how much is it?	quant'è?
when?/do you have?	quando?/avete?

Emergencies

help!	aiuto!
where is the nearest telephone?	dov'è il telefono più vicino
call the police/ doctor/ ambulance	chiamate la polizia/ un medico un'ambulanza
where is the nearest hospital?	dov'è l'ospedale più vicino?

Index

CityPack
Rome

ABOUT THE AUTHOR

Tim Jepson's love of travel began with a busking trip through Europe, and since has taken him from the Umbrian countryside to the Canadian Rockies and the windswept tundra of the Yukon. Future plans include walking the length of Italy and exploring the Arctic and South America. Tim has written several books for the AA, including Explorer guides to *Canada, Rome, Italy, Florence & Tuscany* and *Venice*. Other publications include *Rough Guides* to *Tuscany, Canada* and *The Pacific Northwest*.

AUTHOR AND EDITION REVISER *Tim Jepson* **MANAGING EDITORS** *Apostrophe S Limited*
COVER DESIGN *Tigist Getachew, Fabrizio La Rocca*

A CIP catalogue record for this book is available from the British Library.

ISBN 0 7495 32300

Published by AA Publishing (a trading name of Automobile Association Developments Limited, whose registered office is Millstream, Maidenhead Road, Windsor, Berkshire, SL4 5GD. Registered number 1878835).

© **AUTOMOBILE ASSOCIATION DEVELOPMENTS LIMITED 1996, 1997, 1999, 2002, 2003**
First published 1996. Second edition 1997. Third edition 1999
Fourth edition 2002; Reprinted May 2002. Fifth edition 2003; Reprinted 2004

Colour separation by Daylight Colour Art Pte Ltd, Singapore
Printed and bound by Hang Tai D&P Limited, Hong Kong.

ACKNOWLEDGEMENTS

The Automobile Association would like to thank the following photographers, libraries and associations for their assistance in the preparation of this book.
AKG LONDON 161, 17r, 16c; ARCAID 8/9 (Richard Glover); BRIDGEMAN ART LIBRARY 16r View of the City of Rome, from the Nuremberg Chronicle by Hartmann Schedel (1440–1514) 1493 (woodcut) by German School (15th century) Stapleton Collection, 171 Longitudinal Cross-Section of St Peter's in Rome, plate 26 from Part III of 'The History of the Nations', engraved by G. Lago (engraving) by Italian School (19th century) Private Collection/The Stapleton Collection; ROBERT HARDING PICTURE LIBRARY 11r, 12/3, 191, 19r; HULTON GETTY 17c; PICTOR INTERNATIONAL LTD 101, 18r; SPECTRUM COLOUR LIBRARY 35b; STOCKBYTE 5. The remaining pictures are held in the Association's own library (AA PHOTO LIBRARY) with contributions from: MARTYN ADELMAN 89t; JIM HOLMES cover: Romulus & Remus, back cover: shopping, 1t, 2, 4, 6, 8c, 10/1t, 10/1c, 11tl, 11c, 13tl, 13tr, 13r, 14b, 15, 181, 19tl, 23tc, 24tr, 26t, 27, 28, 31t, 31b, 34, 35t, 39t, 40t, 41, 43b, 46, 48t, 48b, 50b, 56, 57, 59, 62; ALEX KOUPRIANOFF back cover: nightlife, 11tr, 20tc, 20l, 22tr, 24l; SIMON McBRIDE Back cover: Vatican museums, 33; DARIO MITIDIERI 9t, 9br, 10t, 12t, 14tr, 14c, 16t, 18t, 20tl, 20tr, 22tl, 22tc, 23tl, 24r, 25, 30, 36t, 36b, 37, 40b, 45, 47t, 49, 51t, 51b, 52, 55, 60, 61t, 61b, 89b; CLIVE SAWYER cover: Vatican guard, Ponte Sant' Angelo statue, blurred image, 1b, 81, 13c, 21tl, 21, 29t, 29b, 32t, 42, 43t; TONY SOUTER 15t, 20r, 21tr; PETER WILSON cover: Colosseum, Roman figure, Dome of St Peter's. back cover: pizza making, 9r, 14tl, 19tr, 24tl, 26b, 32b, 38, 39b, 44t, 44b, 47b, 50t, 53, 54, 58, 63.

A02166
Maps © Automobile Association Developments Limited 1996, 2002
Transport map © TCS, Aldershot, England